THE KINGFISHER
ATLAS OF THE
ANCIENT
WORLD

Simon Adams

Illustrated by Katherine Baxter

KINGFISHER

BOSTON

KINGFISHER

a Houghton Mifflin Company imprint
222 Berkeley Street
Boston, Massachusetts 02116
www.houghtonmifflinbooks.com

Senior editor: Catherine Brereton
Coordinating editor: Caitlin Doyle
Senior designers: Carol Ann Davis, Malcolm Parchment
Assistant designer: Jack Clucas
Cover designer: Mike Buckley
Consultant: Dr. Miles Russell, Bournemouth University, U.K.
Picture research manager: Cee Weston-Baker
Senior production controller: Lindsey Scott
DTP coordinator: Catherine Hibbert
DTP operator: Claire Cessford
Proofreaders: Sheila Clewley, Essie Cousins

Cartography by: Anderson Geographics Ltd., Warfield, Berkshire, U.K.

First published in 2006
10 9 8 7 6 5 4 3 2 1

1TR/0406/SHENS/CLSN(CLSN)/128MA/C

ISBN-13: 978-07534-5914-0
ISBN-10: 0-7534-5914-0

LIBRARY OF CONGRESS CATALOGING-IN-PUBLICATION DATA
has been applied for.

Printed in Taiwan

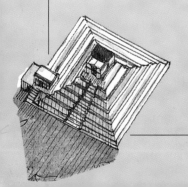

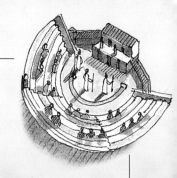

CONTENTS

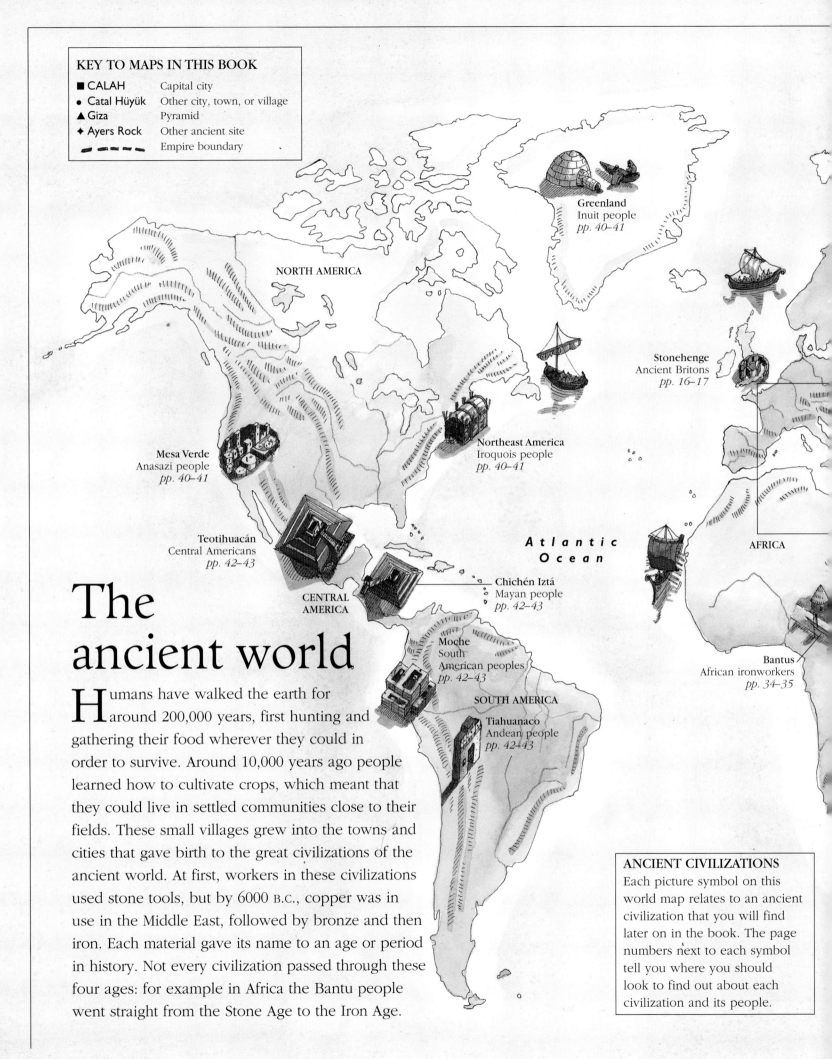

KEY TO MAPS IN THIS BOOK

■ CALAH — Capital city
● Catal Hüyük — Other city, town, or village
▲ Giza — Pyramid
✦ Ayers Rock — Other ancient site
— — — — — Empire boundary

Greenland
Inuit people
pp. 40–41

NORTH AMERICA

Stonehenge
Ancient Britons
pp. 16–17

Mesa Verde
Anasazi people
pp. 40–41

Northeast America
Iroquois people
pp. 40–41

Atlantic
Ocean

AFRICA

Teotihuacán
Central Americans
pp. 42–43

CENTRAL
AMERICA

Chichén Iztá
Mayan people
pp. 42–43

Bantus
African ironworkers
pp. 34–35

Moche
South
American peoples
pp. 42–43

SOUTH AMERICA

Tiahuanaco
Andean people
pp. 42–43

The ancient world

Humans have walked the earth for around 200,000 years, first hunting and gathering their food wherever they could in order to survive. Around 10,000 years ago people learned how to cultivate crops, which meant that they could live in settled communities close to their fields. These small villages grew into the towns and cities that gave birth to the great civilizations of the ancient world. At first, workers in these civilizations used stone tools, but by 6000 B.C., copper was in use in the Middle East, followed by bronze and then iron. Each material gave its name to an age or period in history. Not every civilization passed through these four ages: for example in Africa the Bantu people went straight from the Stone Age to the Iron Age.

ANCIENT CIVILIZATIONS
Each picture symbol on this world map relates to an ancient civilization that you will find later on in the book. The page numbers next to each symbol tell you where you should look to find out about each civilization and its people.

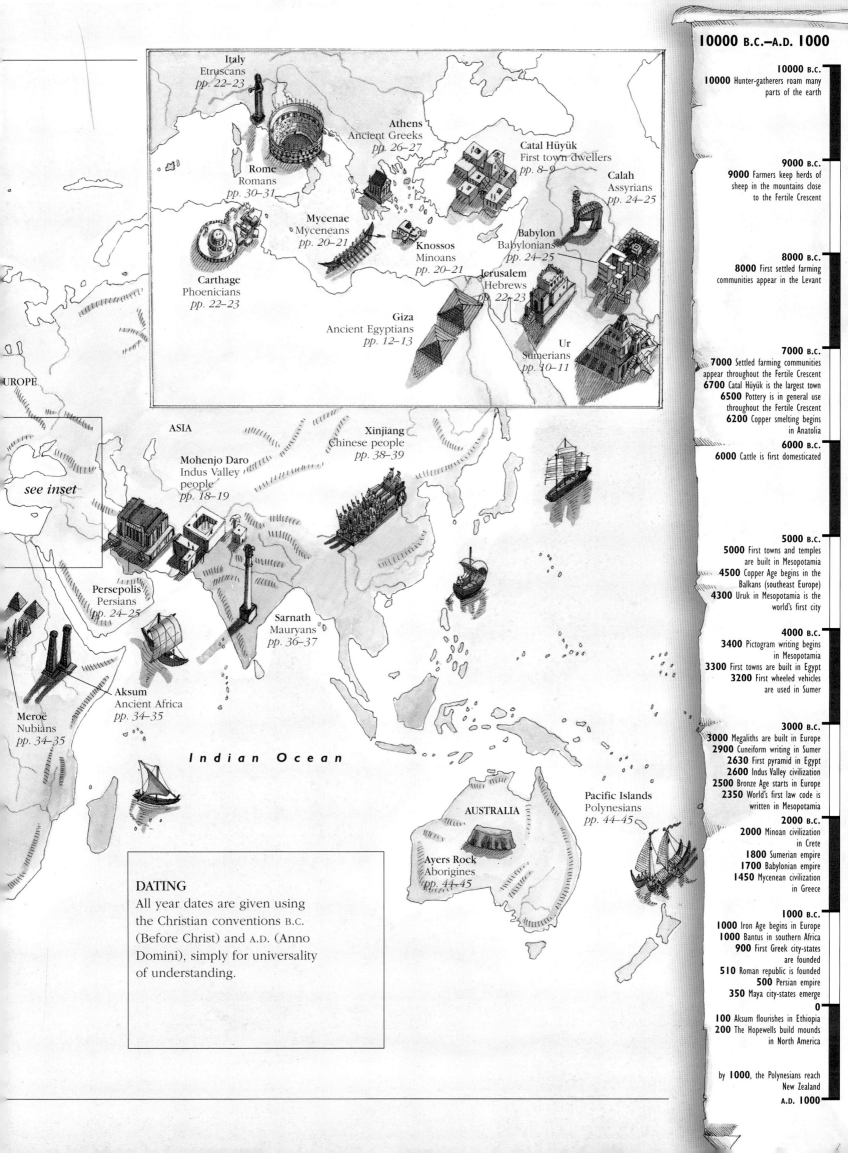

Italy
Etruscans
pp. 22–23

Rome
Romans
pp. 30–31

Athens
Ancient Greeks
pp. 26–27

Catal Hüyük
First town dwellers
pp. 8–9

Calah
Assyrians
pp. 24–25

Mycenae
Myceneans
pp. 20–21

Babylon
Babylonians
pp. 24–25

Knossos
Minoans
pp. 20–21

Carthage
Phoenicians
pp. 22–23

Jerusalem
Hebrews
pp. 22–23

Giza
Ancient Egyptians
pp. 12–13

Ur
Sumerians
pp. 10–11

EUROPE

see inset

ASIA

Xinjiang
Chinese people
pp. 38–39

Mohenjo Daro
Indus Valley
people
pp. 18–19

Persepolis
Persians
pp. 24–25

Sarnath
Mauryans
pp. 36–37

Meroë
Nubians
pp. 34–35

Aksum
Ancient Africa
pp. 34–35

Indian Ocean

Pacific Islands
Polynesians
pp. 44–45

AUSTRALIA

Ayers Rock
Aborigines
pp. 44–45

DATING
All year dates are given using
the Christian conventions B.C.
(Before Christ) and A.D. (Anno
Domini), simply for universality
of understanding.

10000 B.C.–A.D. 1000

10000 B.C.
10000 Hunter-gatherers roam many
parts of the earth

9000 B.C.
9000 Farmers keep herds of
sheep in the mountains close
to the Fertile Crescent

8000 B.C.
8000 First settled farming
communities appear in the Levant

7000 B.C.
7000 Settled farming communities
appear throughout the Fertile Crescent
6700 Catal Hüyük is the largest town
6500 Pottery is in general use
throughout the Fertile Crescent
6200 Copper smelting begins
in Anatolia

6000 B.C.
6000 Cattle is first domesticated

5000 B.C.
5000 First towns and temples
are built in Mesopotamia
4500 Copper Age begins in the
Balkans (southeast Europe)
4300 Uruk in Mesopotamia is the
world's first city

4000 B.C.
3400 Pictogram writing begins
in Mesopotamia
3300 First towns are built in Egypt
3200 First wheeled vehicles
are used in Sumer

3000 B.C.
3000 Megaliths are built in Europe
2900 Cuneiform writing in Sumer
2630 First pyramid in Egypt
2600 Indus Valley civilization
2500 Bronze Age starts in Europe
2350 World's first law code is
written in Mesopotamia

2000 B.C.
2000 Minoan civilization
in Crete
1800 Sumerian empire
1700 Babylonian empire
1450 Mycenean civilization
in Greece

1000 B.C.
1000 Iron Age begins in Europe
1000 Bantus in southern Africa
900 First Greek city-states
are founded
510 Roman republic is founded
500 Persian empire
350 Maya city-states emerge

0
100 Aksum flourishes in Ethiopia
200 The Hopewells build mounds
in North America

by 1000, the Polynesians reach
New Zealand

A.D. 1000

The ancient world:
How we know about the past

Although we cannot travel back in time to speak to the people who lived in the ancient world, we can discover a lot about them based on the objects that they left behind. Buildings, aqueducts and roads, everyday objects, such as pots, tools, coins, and writing implements, and luxury items, such as jewelry and gold ornaments, have all survived to tell their tales. Some buildings, like the Forum in Rome, are still partially standing, while other buildings and smaller objects had been buried for hundreds of years and only recently have been uncovered by archaeologists. All these remains tell us a great deal about the peoples in the ancient world and the lives that they led. From them, we can piece together a picture of what it was like to live in ancient Rome or China, to march with Alexander the Great's army, or to sail the Pacific Ocean, colonizing new islands.

Royal music
This silver lyre—a stringed musical instrument—was made in Ur, modern-day southern Iraq, around 4,500 years ago. It was found in the Royal Cemetery—a lavish burial site where the kings of Ur were buried with their servants. Its incredible craftsmanship and its place of discovery suggest that it was played at the royal court and was buried with the king so that he could continue to enjoy it in the afterlife.

The Forum
The Forum was the political, judicial, and commercial center of Rome and the huge Roman Empire. There, senators met to discuss the important issues of the day and judges tried legal cases. Most of the Forum is now in ruins, but enough of its fine buildings, arches, and monuments survive for us to see just how impressive it must have been when Rome and its armies dominated the Western world.

Cuneiform writing

Priests in the cities of Sumer developed the world's first writing around 3400 B.C. It consisted of simple pictures, and each one represented a word or an idea. By 2900 B.C., this had developed into cuneiform—a writing system that used wedge-shaped marks (*cuneus* is Latin for wedge) that were made by pressing a reed stylus into wet clay.

Hieroglyphics

Around 3300 B.C. the ancient Egyptians began to use a form of writing known as hieroglyphics. This was more complex than Sumerian picture writing and used around 700 different signs to represent different ideas, words, and even individual letters. The hieroglyphs above date from the first century B.C.

Mayan writing

Zapotec scribes in the Americas developed their own unique form of hieroglyphic picture writing in around 800 B.C. Later the Maya used these to develop their own advanced literary language with a "glyph" for every syllable. Many glyphs have only been translated recently.

Hands-on history

Archaeologists study the evidence that is left behind by previous generations. They examine a site or an object, looking for clues that might tell them how old it is, who made it, and why it was found where it was. Even the tiniest scrap of evidence can provide a vital clue, and archaeology can be a long process. Here, an archaeologist is examining a Roman mosaic that was uncovered during the construction of a road in Israel.

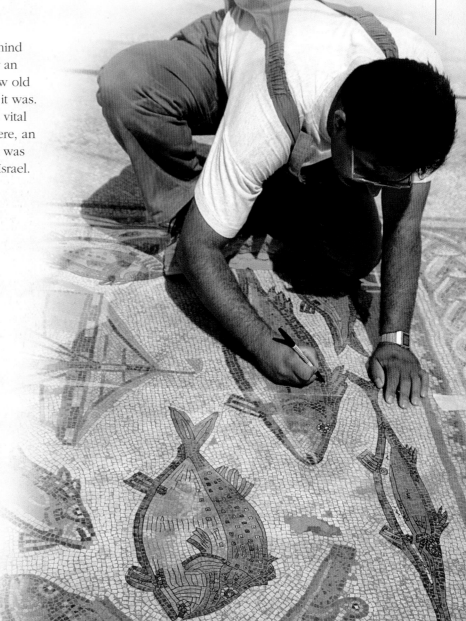

Chinese coins

We use coins every day, but each coin is a piece of history with its own story to tell. Coins show rulers of the time and important symbols, and we can tell a lot about trade based on where they are found. The Chinese have been using coins since the 400s B.C. These were made with a hole in the middle so that they could be kept on a string.

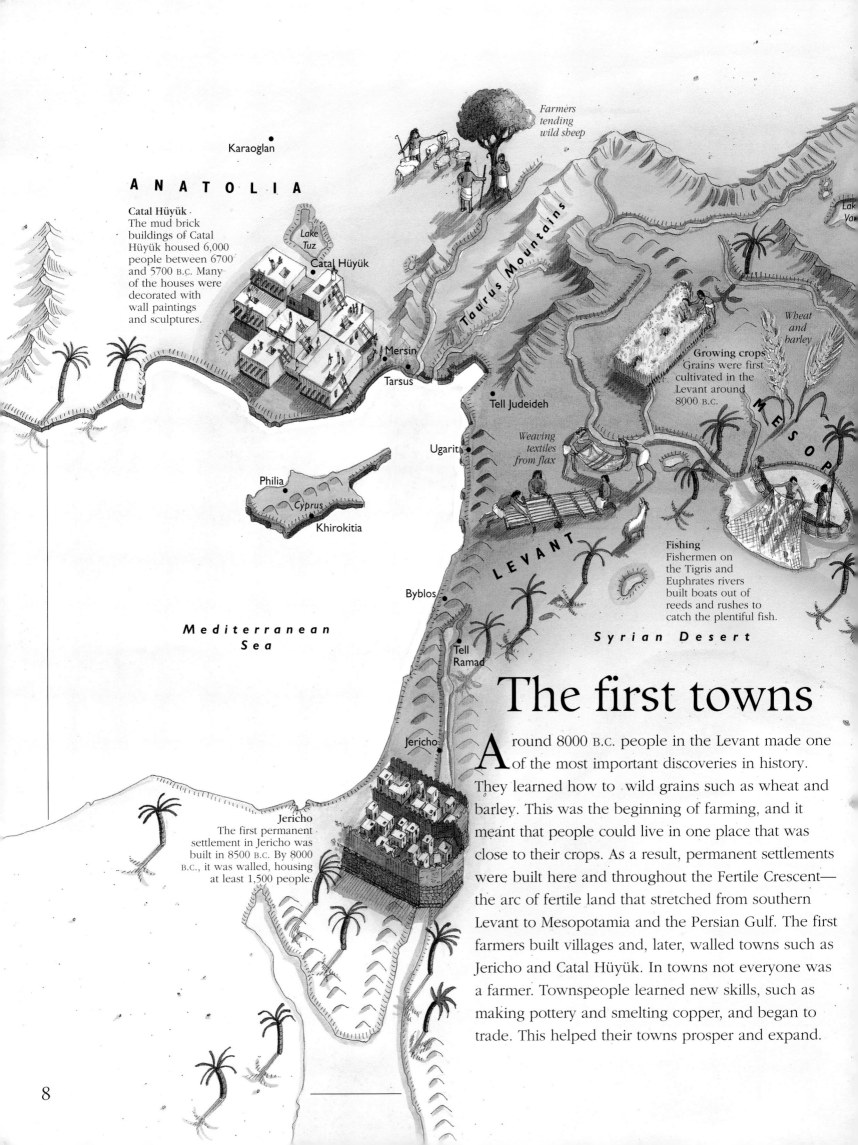

Karaoglan

A N A T O L I A

Catal Hüyük ·
The mud brick
buildings of Catal
Hüyük housed 6,000
people between 6700
and 5700 B.C. Many
of the houses were
decorated with
wall paintings
and sculptures.

Lake Tuz

Catal Hüyük

Mersin

Tarsus

Philia

Cyprus

Khirokitia

Farmers tending wild sheep

Taurus Mountains

Lake Van

Tell Judeideh

Ugarit

Wheat and barley

Growing crops
Grains were first
cultivated in the
Levant around
8000 B.C.

Weaving textiles from flax

M E S O P

L E V A N T

Fishing
Fishermen on
the Tigris and
Euphrates rivers
built boats out of
reeds and rushes to
catch the plentiful fish.

Byblos

Mediterranean Sea

Tell Ramad

Syrian Desert

Jericho

Jericho
The first permanent
settlement in Jericho was
built in 8500 B.C. By 8000
B.C., it was walled, housing
at least 1,500 people.

The first towns

A round 8000 B.C. people in the Levant made one
of the most important discoveries in history.
They learned how to wild grains such as wheat and
barley. This was the beginning of farming, and it
meant that people could live in one place that was
close to their crops. As a result, permanent settlements
were built here and throughout the Fertile Crescent—
the arc of fertile land that stretched from southern
Levant to Mesopotamia and the Persian Gulf. The first
farmers built villages and, later, walled towns such as
Jericho and Catal Hüyük. In towns not everyone was
a farmer. Townspeople learned new skills, such as
making pottery and smelting copper, and began to
trade. This helped their towns prosper and expand.

Plows helping farmers cultivate the land

Pottery
Potters in Hassuna learned how to fire pottery in a kiln around 6000 B.C.

Smelting copper
Smelting copper to make weapons and tools reached southern Mesopotamia before 4000 B.C.

Irrigating the land
Farmers began building canals and irrigation ditches in Mesopotamia around 5500 B.C.

Local industries
A pottery industry that used local clay built up in Susa and nearby towns in the 4000s B.C.

Temples
The people of southern Mesopotamia built large temples and grain storehouses in Uruk and other towns after 5000 B.C.

Eridu
Eridu, the oldest town in southern Mesopotamia, had a population of around 5,000 in 4000 B.C. It traded pottery and other goods with Arabia.

The development of farming

The first peoples were hunter-gatherers who found food by killing wild animals and collecting wild fruits, nuts, and grains. In the Levant wild crops were so plentiful that by around 10000 B.C. people did not need to move around in order to find food. Slowly they learned how to plant and grow wild grains so that the crops would produce more food and be easier to harvest. Early farmers domesticated sheep, goats, pigs, and cattle, and by 6000 B.C., they could feed a large, settled urban population.

Map labels

Yanik Tepe
Lake Urmia
Tepe Gawra
Hassuna
Tell Umm Dabaghiyeh
Tigris
Samarra
Tell Al-Sawwan
Choga Mami
Tell Uqair
Nippur
Euphrates
Tepe Guran
Susa
Ali Kosh
Uruk
Tel Awayli
Eridu
M-E-S-O-P-O-T-A-M-I-A
Zagros Mountains
Persian Gulf

0   200km
0   100 miles

Timeline

10000 B.C.
10000 Farmers in the Levant first build wooden huts with stone foundations

9500 B.C.

9000 B.C.
9000 Wild sheep herds are first kept by farmers in the Taurus and Zagros mountains

8500 B.C.

8000 B.C.
8000 Barley and wheat are cultivated in the Levant, allowing settled farming communities to develop
8000 The walled city of Jericho has 1,500 inhabitants

7500 B.C.
7500 Flax is first used for textiles

7000 B.C.
7000 Settled farming communities flourish throughout the Fertile Crescent
7000 Goats, sheep, and later pigs are domesticated in the Taurus Mountains
6700 Çatal Hüyük, with 6,000 inhabitants, is the largest town

6500 B.C.
6500 Pottery comes into general use
6200 Copper smelting begins in Çatal Hüyük

6000 B.C.
6000 Cattle are first domesticated
6000 Kiln-fired pottery develops in Hassuna

5500 B.C.
5500 Irrigation allows farming communities to flourish in the arid soil of Mesopotamia

5000 B.C.
5000 The first towns and temples are built in Mesopotamia

4500 B.C.
4500 The plow, sail, and potter's wheel are in common use in Mesopotamia
4300 Copper working for tools and weapons begins in Mesopotamia
4000 Sheep are bred for wool

4000 B.C.

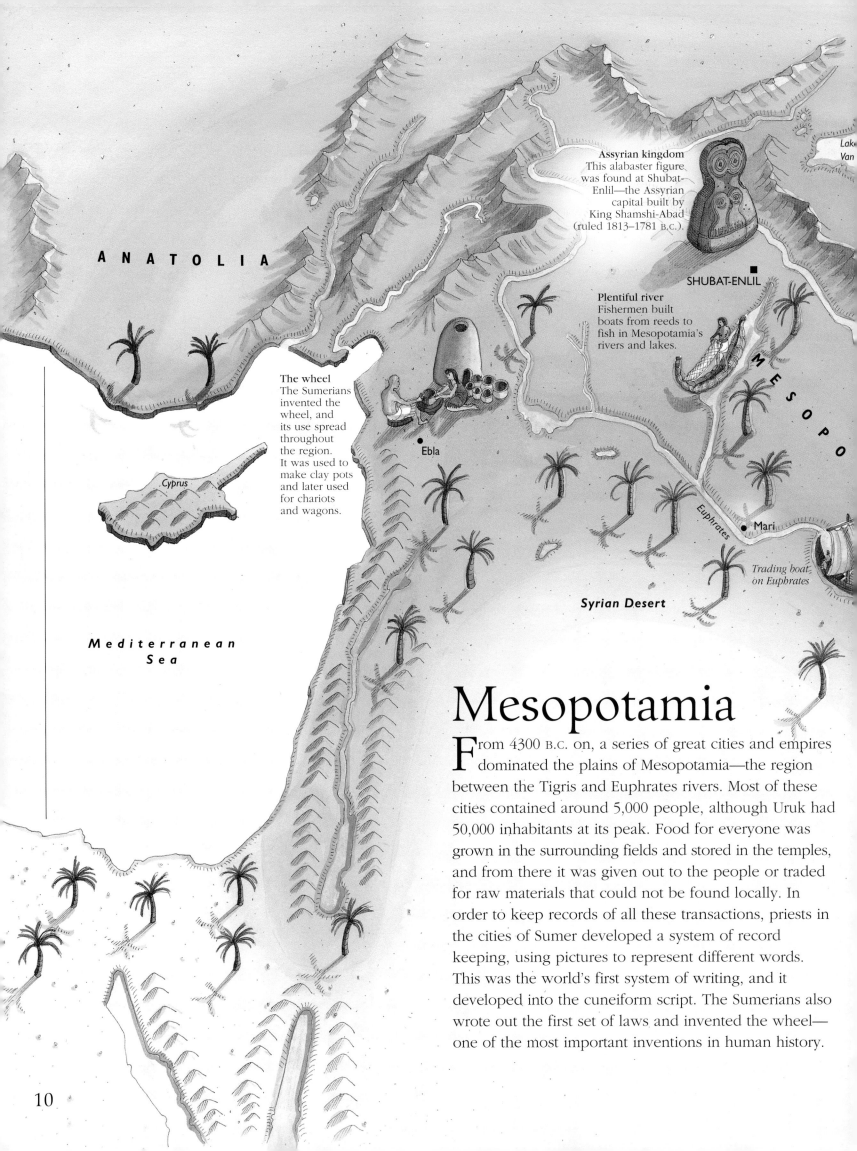

Assyrian kingdom
This alabaster figure was found at Shubat-Enlil—the Assyrian capital built by King Shamshi-Abad (ruled 1813–1781 B.C.).

SHUBAT-ENLIL

Plentiful river
Fishermen built boats from reeds to fish in Mesopotamia's rivers and lakes.

A N A T O L I A

The wheel
The Sumerians invented the wheel, and its use spread throughout the region. It was used to make clay pots and later used for chariots and wagons.

M E S O P O

Cyprus

• Ebla

Euphrates

• Mari

Trading boat on Euphrates

Syrian Desert

Mediterranean Sea

Lake Van

Mesopotamia

From 4300 B.C. on, a series of great cities and empires dominated the plains of Mesopotamia—the region between the Tigris and Euphrates rivers. Most of these cities contained around 5,000 people, although Uruk had 50,000 inhabitants at its peak. Food for everyone was grown in the surrounding fields and stored in the temples, and from there it was given out to the people or traded for raw materials that could not be found locally. In order to keep records of all these transactions, priests in the cities of Sumer developed a system of record keeping, using pictures to represent different words. This was the world's first system of writing, and it developed into the cuneiform script. The Sumerians also wrote out the first set of laws and invented the wheel— one of the most important inventions in human history.

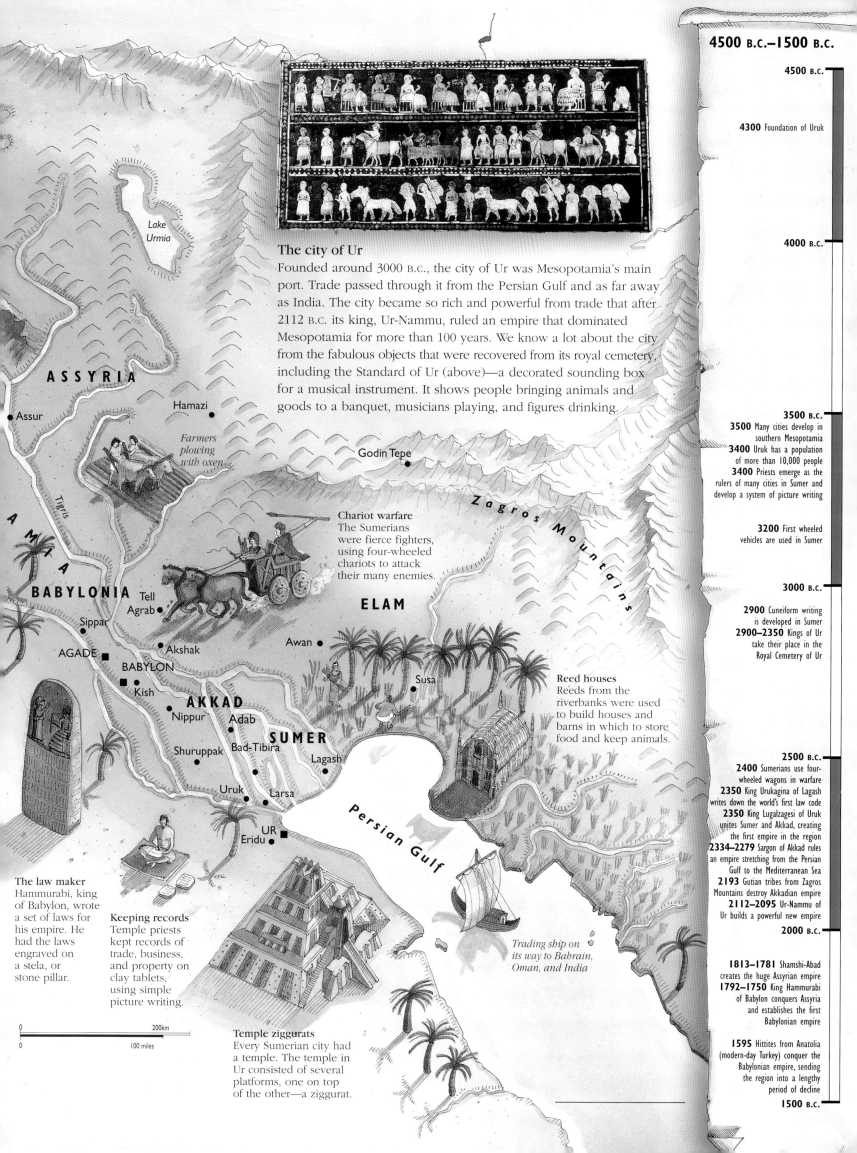

The city of Ur

Founded around 3000 B.C., the city of Ur was Mesopotamia's main port. Trade passed through it from the Persian Gulf and as far away as India. The city became so rich and powerful from trade that after 2112 B.C. its king, Ur-Nammu, ruled an empire that dominated Mesopotamia for more than 100 years. We know a lot about the city from the fabulous objects that were recovered from its royal cemetery, including the Standard of Ur (above)—a decorated sounding box for a musical instrument. It shows people bringing animals and goods to a banquet, musicians playing, and figures drinking.

Farmers plowing with oxen

Chariot warfare
The Sumerians were fierce fighters, using four-wheeled chariots to attack their many enemies.

Reed houses
Reeds from the riverbanks were used to build houses and barns in which to store food and keep animals.

The law maker
Hammurabi, king of Babylon, wrote a set of laws for his empire. He had the laws engraved on a stela, or stone pillar.

Keeping records
Temple priests kept records of trade, business, and property on clay tablets, using simple picture writing.

Trading ship on its way to Bahrain, Oman, and India

Temple ziggurats
Every Sumerian city had a temple. The temple in Ur consisted of several platforms, one on top of the other—a ziggurat.

Map labels

- Lake Urmia
- ASSYRIA
- Assur
- Hamazi
- Godin Tepe
- Zagros Mountains
- Tigris
- MITANNI
- BABYLONIA
- Tell Agrab
- Sippar
- AGADE
- BABYLON
- Kish
- Akshak
- ELAM
- Awan
- Susa
- AKKAD
- Nippur
- Adab
- Bad-Tibira
- SUMER
- Shuruppak
- Lagash
- Uruk
- Larsa
- UR
- Eridu
- Persian Gulf

0 — 200km
0 — 100 miles

Timeline

4500 B.C.

4300 Foundation of Uruk

4000 B.C.

3500 B.C.
3500 Many cities develop in southern Mesopotamia
3400 Uruk has a population of more than 10,000 people
3400 Priests emerge as the rulers of many cities in Sumer and develop a system of picture writing

3200 First wheeled vehicles are used in Sumer

3000 B.C.
2900 Cuneiform writing is developed in Sumer
2900–2350 Kings of Ur take their place in the Royal Cemetery of Ur

2500 B.C.
2400 Sumerians use four-wheeled wagons in warfare
2350 King Urukagina of Lagash writes down the world's first law code
2350 King Lugalzagesi of Uruk unites Sumer and Akkad, creating the first empire in the region
2334–2279 Sargon of Akkad rules an empire stretching from the Persian Gulf to the Mediterranean Sea
2193 Gutian tribes from Zagros Mountains destroy Akkadian empire
2112–2095 Ur-Nammu of Ur builds a powerful new empire

2000 B.C.
1813–1781 Shamshi-Abad creates the huge Assyrian empire
1792–1750 King Hammurabi of Babylon conquers Assyria and establishes the first Babylonian empire

1595 Hittites from Anatolia (modern-day Turkey) conquer the Babylonian empire, sending the region into a lengthy period of decline

1500 B.C.

Ancient Egypt

For more than 3,000 years the Egyptians, ruled by kings called pharaohs, established a remarkable civilization along the banks of the Nile river—Egypt's main highway. People and goods traveled along it, and it supplied fresh water for humans and animals and irrigated the crops. Surplus food, linen, and papyrus were traded throughout the region in return for silver, copper, tin, timber, horses, and human slaves, making Egypt a wealthy and powerful nation. The Egyptians were one of the first people to invent a system of picture writing, known as hieroglyphics. They were also skilled builders, constructing magnificent stone palaces, temples, and pyramid-shaped tombs—many of which still survive today.

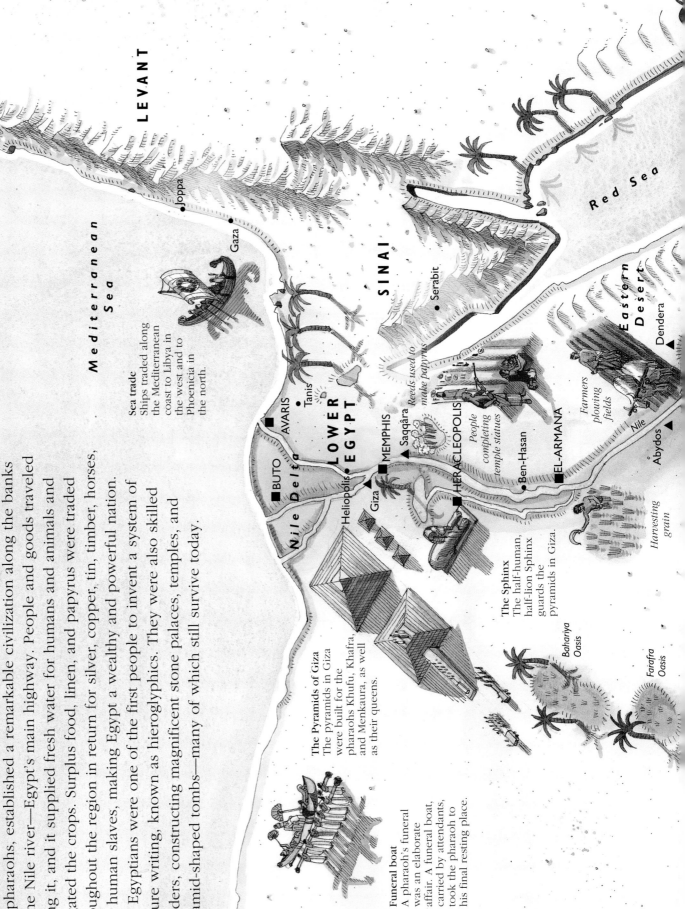

LEVANT

Joppa

Gaza

Mediterranean Sea

Sea trade
Ships traded along the Mediterranean coast to Libya in the west and to Phoenicia in the north.

Red Sea

SINAI

Serabit

Eastern Desert

Dendera

Abydos

Harvesting grain

Nile

EL-ARMANA

Farmers plowing fields

Ben-Hasan

HERACLEOPOLIS
People completing temple statues

Faiyum Oasis

Bahariya Oasis

Farafra Oasis

Saqqâra

MEMPHIS

Heliopolis

Giza

LOWER EGYPT

Tanis

AVARIS

BUTO

Nile Delta

The Sphinx
The half-human, half-lion Sphinx guards the pyramids in Giza.

The Pyramids of Giza
The pyramids in Giza were built for the pharaohs Khufu, Khafra, and Menkaura, as well as their queens.

Reeds used to make papyrus

Funeral boat
A pharaoh's funeral was an elaborate affair. A funeral boat, carried by attendants, took the pharaoh to his final resting place.

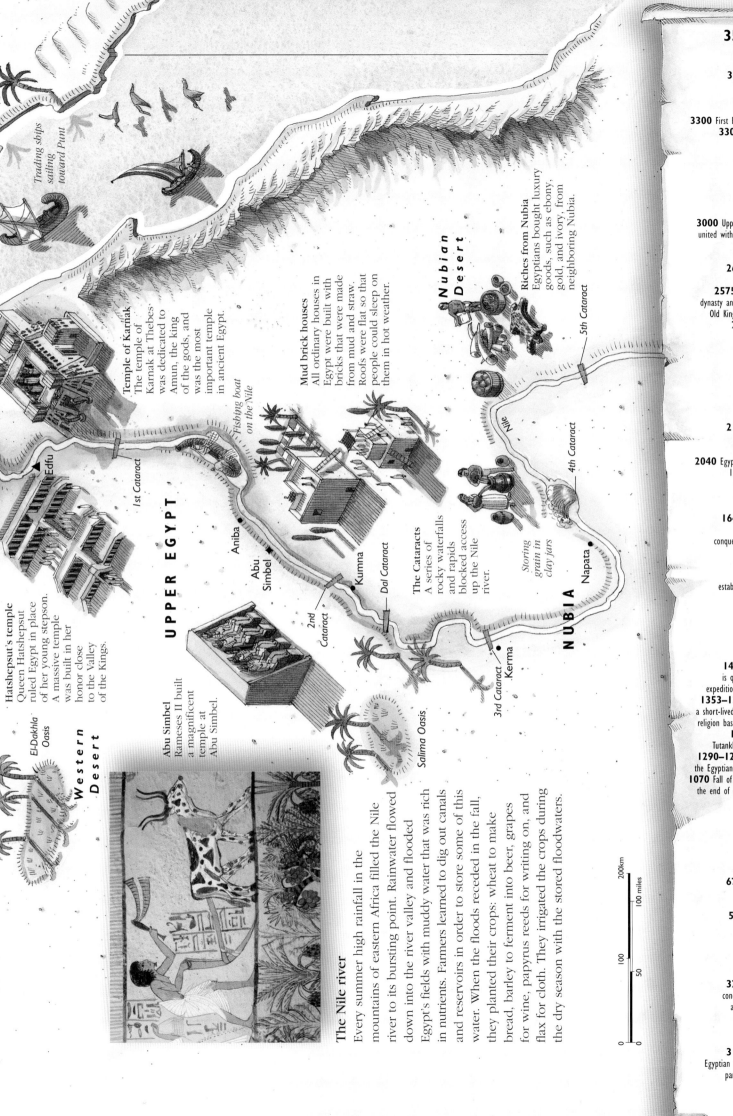

3500 B.C.
3500 Farming flourishes in the Nile Valley

3300 First Egyptian towns are built
3300–3000 Hieroglyphic script is developed

3000 B.C.
3000 Upper and Lower Egypt are united with the capital at Memphis
2920 First dynasty of kings begins to rule
2630 First step pyramid are built at Saqq ra
2575 Snofru founds the 4th dynasty and establishes a powerful Old Kingdom based at Memphis
2550 Khufu builds the Great Pyramid in Gi a

2500 B.C.

2134 Old Kingdom ends as Egypt divides into two rival kingdoms
2040 Egypt is reunified under the 11th dynasty, establishing the Middle Kingdom

2000 B.C.
1640–1550 The Hyksos people from the Levant conquer and rule Lower Egypt

1550 Ahmose founds the 18th dynasty and establishes the New Kingdom

1500 B.C.
1473–1458 Hatshepsut is queen and sends a naval expedition to Punt in east Africa
1353–1335 Akhenaten creates a short-lived monotheistic (one-god) religion based on Aten, the sun-god
1333–1323 Reign of Tutankhamen, the boy pharaoh
1290–1224 Rameses II extends the Egyptian empire into the Levant
1070 Fall of the 21st dynasty marks the end of effective Egyptian power

1000 B.C.

671–651 The Assyrians occupy Egypt

525–523 The Persians briefly conquer Egypt

500 B.C.

323 Alexander the Great conquers Egypt, establishing a new Ptolemaic dynasty

3 Death of Cleopatra, last Egyptian pharaoh; Egypt becomes part of the Roman Empire

0

Trading ships sailing toward Punt

Temple of Karnak
The temple of Karnak at Thebes was dedicated to Amun, the king of the gods, and was the most important temple in ancient Egypt.

Mud brick houses
All ordinary houses in Egypt were built with bricks that were made from mud and straw. Roofs were flat so that people could sleep on them in hot weather.

Riches from Nubia
Egyptians bought luxury goods, such as ebony, gold, and ivory, from neighboring Nubia.

Nubian Desert

5th Cataract

Fishing boat on the Nile

UPPER EGYPT

1st Cataract

Edfu

Nile

4th Cataract

Aniba

Abu Simbel

Kumna

Dal Cataract

The Cataracts
A series of rocky waterfalls and rapids blocked access up the Nile river.

Storing grain in clay jars

NUBIA

Napata

2nd Cataract

Hatshepsut's temple
Queen Hatshepsut ruled Egypt in place of her young stepson. A massive temple was built in her honor close to the Valley of the Kings.

El-Dakhla Oasis

Western Desert

Abu Simbel
Rameses II built a magnificent temple at Abu Simbel.

Salima Oasis

3rd Cataract
Kerma

The Nile river

Every summer high rainfall in the mountains of eastern Africa filled the Nile river to its bursting point. Rainwater flowed down into the river valley and flooded Egypt's fields with muddy water that was rich in nutrients. Farmers learned to dig out canals and reservoirs in order to store some of this water. When the floods receded in the fall, they planted their crops: wheat to make bread, barley to ferment into beer, grapes for wine, papyrus reeds for writing on, and flax for cloth. They irrigated the crops during the dry season with the stored floodwaters.

200km

100 miles

100

50

Ancient Egypt:
Preparing for the afterlife

The ancient Egyptians had a strong belief in the afterlife, since they dreaded the day that their own world might come to an end. They developed an elaborate method of embalming and mummifying bodies so that they would last forever. Important people, such as the pharaoh (king), were buried along with their belongings inside of a great pyramid. Later the pharaohs were buried in tombs in the Valley of the Kings. Although most of these pyramids and tombs have been robbed of their contents, a few have survived intact, giving us a good idea about the Egyptian way of life and death more than 3,000 years ago.

Mummification

After death the body was taken to a place known as the Beautiful House to be preserved. Embalmers removed the internal organs, leaving the heart so that it could be weighed in the afterlife. The body was then covered with the crystals of the chemical natron, in order to dry it out and prevent decay. After around 40 days the body was ready for the next stage. It was stuffed with dry materials, such as sawdust or leaves, and tightly wrapped up in linen bandages. Finally, it was put into a stone or wooden coffin. Lowly people were buried in graveyards, but important people, such as the boy pharaoh Tutankhamen (right; ruled 1333–1323 B.C.) were placed into an elaborate container. This was made up of layers—each one beautifully decorated inside with gods of the underworld, and outside with hieroglyphs and magic symbols. Once it was safely in its coffin, the body was ready for the afterlife.

Weighing the heart

The Egyptians believed in an underworld called Duat, which contained lakes of fire and poisonous snakes. Spells to ward off these dangers, and others, were written on the coffin. The biggest danger was in the Hall of Two Truths, where a person's heart was weighed against past deeds (left). There the dead person was asked about their life. If they told the truth, they were allowed to pass into the afterlife.

Inner life

Embalmers removed the dead person's internal organs by making a cut in the left side of the body with a flint knife and extracting the liver, lungs, intestines, and stomach. These were then dried, wrapped up in linen, and each one was placed in a separate canopic jar, bearing the head of one of the four gods known as the Sons of Horus.

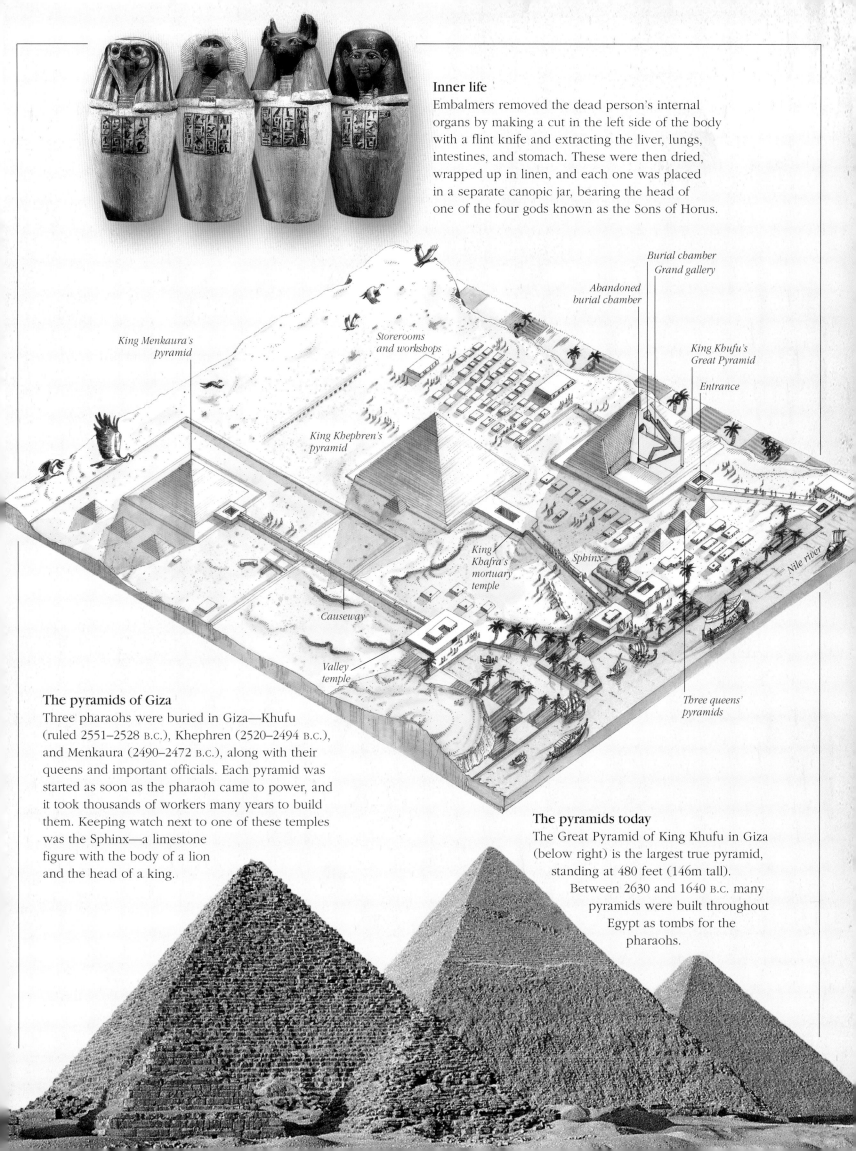

King Menkaura's pyramid

Storerooms and workshops

Abandoned burial chamber

Burial chamber
Grand gallery

King Khufu's Great Pyramid

Entrance

King Khephren's pyramid

King Khafra's mortuary temple

Sphinx

Nile river

Causeway

Valley temple

Three queens' pyramids

The pyramids of Giza

Three pharaohs were buried in Giza—Khufu (ruled 2551–2528 B.C.), Khephren (2520–2494 B.C.), and Menkaura (2490–2472 B.C.), along with their queens and important officials. Each pyramid was started as soon as the pharaoh came to power, and it took thousands of workers many years to build them. Keeping watch next to one of these temples was the Sphinx—a limestone figure with the body of a lion and the head of a king.

The pyramids today

The Great Pyramid of King Khufu in Giza (below right) is the largest true pyramid, standing at 480 feet (146m tall). Between 2630 and 1640 B.C. many pyramids were built throughout Egypt as tombs for the pharaohs.

Ancient Europe

Farming began in southeastern Europe during the Neolithic Age—around 6000 B.C.—and slowly spread throughout Europe over the next 2,000 years. Farming allowed people to settle down and build houses and villages to live in, but the real advance came with the use of copper, bronze, and then iron. These metals could be made into tools and weapons, as well as items such as jewelry and other ornamental or ceremonial objects. In many places chiefs and other important people were buried in megalithic (giant stone) tombs with beautiful offerings to the gods next to them. People built massive circles and rows of standing stones and circular earth structures known as henges. Some of these line up with the sun and stars at certain times of the year, indicating a detailed knowledge of the calendar and astronomy.

Ancient sites
The key on page 4 tells you that places that are marked with a diamond are not cities, towns, or villages but other types of ancient sites. On this map these sites are stone circles, rows of standing stones, or stone tombs. An example is ✦ Stonehenge.

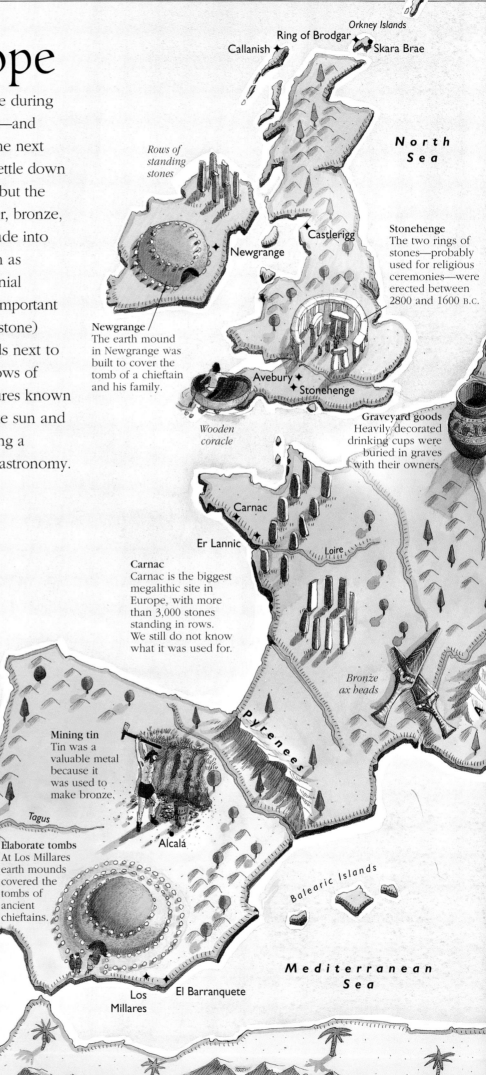

Callanish

Orkney Islands
Ring of Brodgar
Skara Brae

North Sea

Rows of standing stones

Castlerigg

Newgrange

Stonehenge
The two rings of stones—probably used for religious ceremonies—were erected between 2800 and 1600 B.C.

Newgrange
The earth mound in Newgrange was built to cover the tomb of a chieftain and his family.

Avebury ✦ Stonehenge

Wooden coracle

Graveyard goods
Heavily decorated drinking cups were buried in graves with their owners.

Carnac

Er Lannic

Loire

Carnac
Carnac is the biggest megalithic site in Europe, with more than 3,000 stones standing in rows. We still do not know what it was used for.

Bronze ax heads

Pyrenees

Atlantic Ocean

Mining tin
Tin was a valuable metal because it was used to make bronze.

Tagus

Alcalá

Elaborate tombs
At Los Millares earth mounds covered the tombs of ancient chieftains.

Balearic Islands

Mediterranean Sea

Los Millares

El Barranquete

| 0 | 500 | 1000km |
| 0 | 250 | 500 miles |

SCANDINAVIA

Rickeby

Ålborg

Trundholm

Kivic

Bronze Age burial mound

Collecting amber for jewelry

Celtic weapons
The Celts made elaborate shields and other items out of bronze.

Elbe

Rhine

Helmsdorf

Leubingen

Wasserburg

Lake villages
Bronze Age peoples often built villages off the shores of a lake for defense.

Longhouse for people and animals

House raised up on wooden pillars

Barca

Carpathian Mountains

Cutting down trees for timber and fuel

Danube

A l p s

Making bronze
Smiths mixed together hot tin and copper in a mold to make bronze—a stronger metal.

Corsica

Sardinia

A d r i a t i c   S e a

Milking goats

Black Sea

Greek cargo ship

Sicily

Stentinello

A e g e a n   S e a

Life at home
Wood was plentiful, so most people in Europe lived in wooden longhouses. The ruins of these houses are very rare, and we know very little about what they were like inside. The exception is on the treeless Orkney Islands, where, around 3000 B.C. at Skara Brae, the people built an entire village out of stone. Their houses were covered with stone and turf and contained stone cupboards, fireplaces, beds, and boxes.

6000 B.C.–500 B.C.

6000 B.C.
6000 Farming is established in southeastern Europe during the Neolithic Age

5500 B.C.

5000 B.C.
5000 Farming spreads around the Mediterranean

4500 B.C.
4500 Copper smelting begins in southeastern Europe—start of the Copper Age
4500 Plows are first used on farms in southeastern Europe
4300 First megalithic tombs are built

4000 B.C.
4000 Horses are first domesticated in Europe

3500 B.C.

3200 First wheeled vehicles are in use in the Balkans

3000 B.C.
3000 Skara Brae stone village is built in the Orkney Islands
3000 Megalithic stone circles and rows, as well as earth-mound burial tombs, are first built in western Europe
2800 Work begins on the construction of Stonehenge

2500 B.C.
2500 Tin is first added to copper in central Europe to make bronze—star the Bronze Age in Europe

2000 B.C.
2000 Hill forts and lake villages are built in central Europe
2000 Metal ores and amber are now traded across all of Europe

1500 B.C.

1200 The Celts flourish in central Europe

1000 B.C.
1000 Iron is first used in Greece—start of the Iron Age in Europe
750 Celts begin to settle in western Europe
700 Iron is in widespread use throughout Europe

500 B.C.

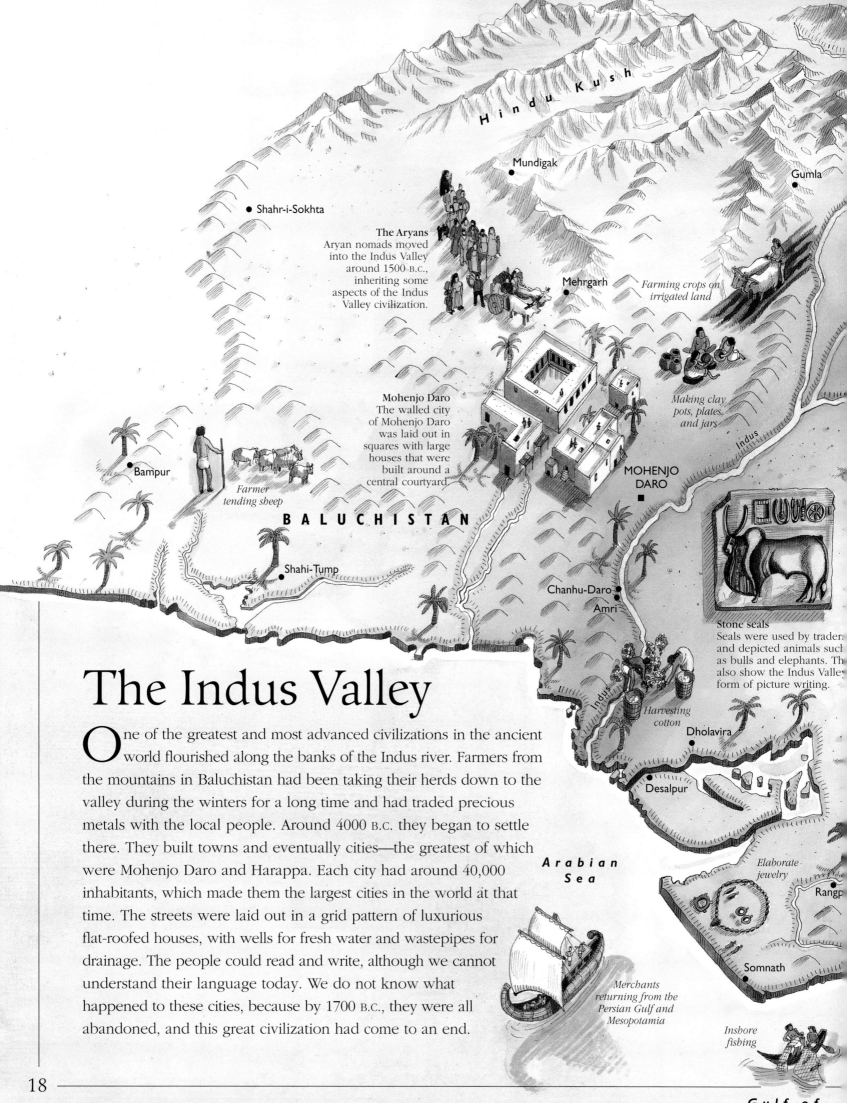

Hindu Kush

Mundigak

Gumla

Shahr-i-Sokhta

The Aryans
Aryan nomads moved into the Indus Valley around 1500 B.C., inheriting some aspects of the Indus Valley civilization.

Mehrgarh

Farming crops on irrigated land

Mohenjo Daro
The walled city of Mohenjo Daro was laid out in squares with large houses that were built around a central courtyard.

Making clay pots, plates, and jars

Indus

MOHENJO DARO

Bampur

Farmer tending sheep

B A L U C H I S T A N

Shahi-Tump

Stone seals
Seals were used by trader and depicted animals such as bulls and elephants. Th also show the Indus Valley form of picture writing.

Chanhu-Daro

Amri

Indus

Harvesting cotton

Dholavira

The Indus Valley

One of the greatest and most advanced civilizations in the ancient world flourished along the banks of the Indus river. Farmers from the mountains in Baluchistan had been taking their herds down to the valley during the winters for a long time and had traded precious metals with the local people. Around 4000 B.C. they began to settle there. They built towns and eventually cities—the greatest of which were Mohenjo Daro and Harappa. Each city had around 40,000 inhabitants, which made them the largest cities in the world at that time. The streets were laid out in a grid pattern of luxurious flat-roofed houses, with wells for fresh water and wastepipes for drainage. The people could read and write, although we cannot understand their language today. We do not know what happened to these cities, because by 1700 B.C., they were all abandoned, and this great civilization had come to an end.

Desalpur

Arabian Sea

Elaborate jewelry

Rangp

Somnath

Merchants returning from the Persian Gulf and Mesopotamia

Inshore fishing

Gulf of Khabhat

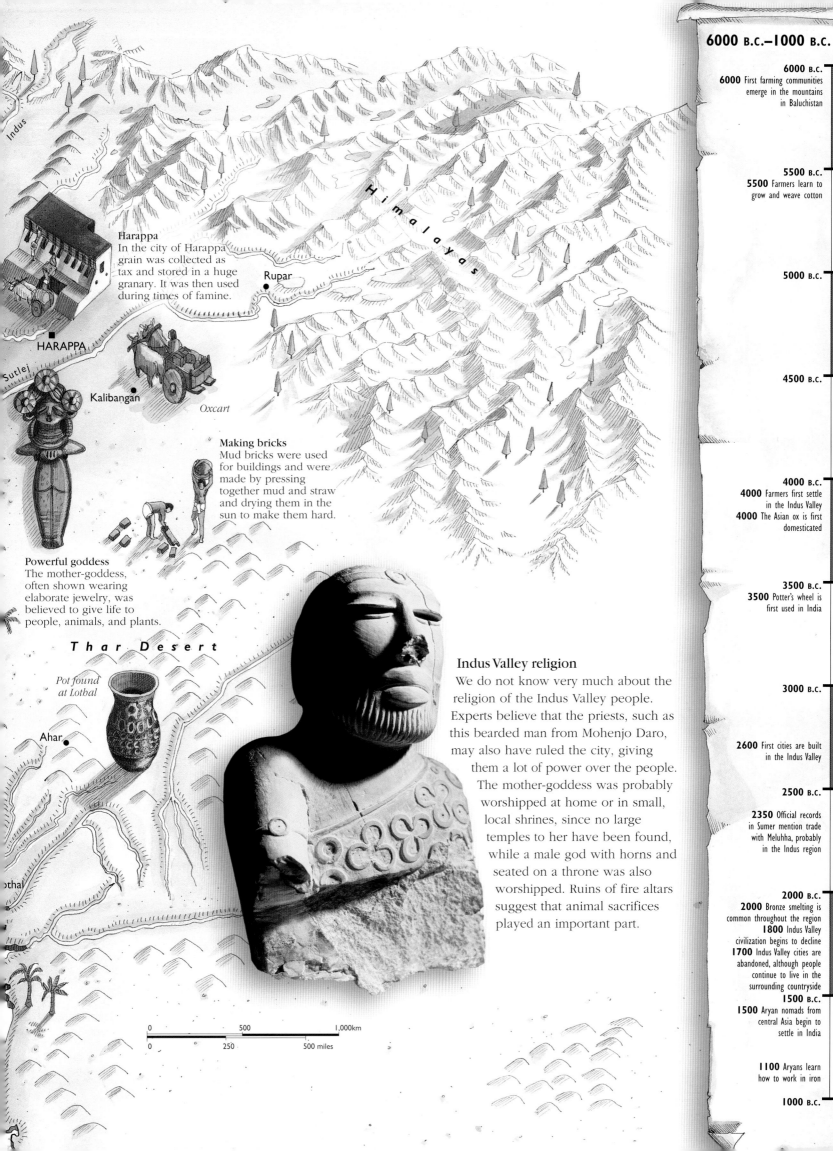

Harappa
In the city of Harappa grain was collected as tax and stored in a huge granary. It was then used during times of famine.

HARAPPA

Kalibangan

Oxcart

Making bricks
Mud bricks were used for buildings and were made by pressing together mud and straw and drying them in the sun to make them hard.

Powerful goddess
The mother-goddess, often shown wearing elaborate jewelry, was believed to give life to people, animals, and plants.

Thar Desert

Pot found at Lothal

Ahar

Rupar

Himalayas

Indus

Sutlej

Indus Valley religion

We do not know very much about the religion of the Indus Valley people. Experts believe that the priests, such as this bearded man from Mohenjo Daro, may also have ruled the city, giving them a lot of power over the people. The mother-goddess was probably worshipped at home or in small, local shrines, since no large temples to her have been found, while a male god with horns and seated on a throne was also worshipped. Ruins of fire altars suggest that animal sacrifices played an important part.

6000 B.C.–1000 B.C.

6000 B.C.
6000 First farming communities emerge in the mountains in Baluchistan

5500 B.C.
5500 Farmers learn to grow and weave cotton

5000 B.C.

4500 B.C.

4000 B.C.
4000 Farmers first settle in the Indus Valley
4000 The Asian ox is first domesticated

3500 B.C.
3500 Potter's wheel is first used in India

3000 B.C.

2600 First cities are built in the Indus Valley

2500 B.C.
2350 Official records in Sumer mention trade with Meluhha, probably in the Indus region

2000 B.C.
2000 Bronze smelting is common throughout the region
1800 Indus Valley civilization begins to decline
1700 Indus Valley cities are abandoned, although people continue to live in the surrounding countryside
1500 B.C.
1500 Aryan nomads from central Asia begin to settle in India

1100 Aryans learn how to work in iron

1000 B.C.

Olive harvesting

Karditsa

Iolkos

Mycenae's Lion Gate
This magnificent stone gate was the main entrance to the city and one of the only ways through its walls.

Farming wheat

Royal graves
Mycenean leaders were buried in shaft graves. The grave at Mycenae contained bronze weapons and luxury goods.

Orchomenos Gla

Khalkis

Lefkandi

Dyme

Thebes

Marathon

Athens

PELOPONNESE

Mycenae

Tiryns Dendra

Height of power
Mycenean cities were built on hilltops and surrounded by strong defensive walls.

Menelaion

Vaphio

Pylos

Minoans and Myceneans

The Minoan civilization began on the island of Crete more than 4,000 years ago. By 2000 B.C., the Minoans had built several cities with impressive palaces. The capital, Knossos, had the most incredible palace complex—with temples, storerooms, workshops, and everything that was needed for daily life. The riches that were gained from trade meant that the Minoans were envied by the neighboring Myceneans. These people had migrated to Greece from the Balkans in around 2000 B.C. Their civilization grew up from a series of hillside villages to fortified city-states. The two cultures lived side by side for a while, and both developed their own forms of writing. In 1626 B.C. a huge earthquake was caused by a volcanic eruption on Thera, which damaged the Minoan cities. Shortly afterward, Crete was invaded and colonized by the Myceneans, and Mycenean civilization dominated the region until it too was conquered in around 1200 B.C.

Mycenean warship heading toward Crete

Mycenean trading ship going to Sicily

Wealthy Minoan people

Ch

Trojan horse
Agamemnon, the leader of the Greeks who conquered Troy, was almost certainly a Mycenean king.

Troy
Lemnos
Poliochni

Minoan trading ship

Aegean Sea

Lesbos

Chios

Andros

Serraglia
Kos

Delos

Páros   Naxos

ilos
Phylakopi

Volcano erupting on Thera

Thera

Luxurious palace
The Palace of Knossos had royal apartments, courtyards, underfloor heating, sunken baths, running water, and lush gardens.

Knossos
Phaistos **CRETE**   Zakros

Legendary beast
For the Minoans and the Myceneans, the bull was a sacred symbol of power. This wall painting from the Palace of Knossos shows the sport of bull-leaping. Athletes would vault over the bull's horns, symbolizing the mastering of its strength. Bulls were so important to Minoan life that their most famous legend is of the Minotaur—a terrible monster that was half man and half bull and lived in an underground maze in Knossos.

Merchants from Miletos trading with Hittites

Miletos

ANATOLIA

Ialyssos
Rhodes
Lindos

0   100   200km
0   50   100 miles

2000 B.C.
2000 Minoans begin to build cities and palaces on Crete and create the first states in Europe
2000 Minoans develop their own hieroglyphic (picture) writing
2000 Greek-speaking Myceneans move south from the Balkans to settle in Greece

1900 B.C.

1800 B.C.

1700 B.C.
1700 After a large fire, possibly caused by warfare, Minoan palaces are rebuilt. Knossos becomes the main city
1650 Myceneans build fortified towns in mainland Greece and begin to create small kingdoms
1626 A volcano erupts on Thera; earthquakes and ash falls engulf Crete

1600 B.C.
1600 Myceneans begin to bury their dead leaders in shaft graves

1500 B.C.
1450 Myceneans conquer Crete and end Minoan civilization
1450 Myceneans begin to settle in colonies such as Miletos on the Anatolian coast
1450 Myceneans develop Linear B script—the origin of modern-day Greek writing

1400 B.C.

1300 B.C.
1250 The city of Troy is attacked twice around this time, starting the Greek legend of the Trojan Wars

1200 B.C.
1200 Sea peoples from Anatolia attack Greece and end Mycenean civilization. Many Myceneans move to Anatolia and Cyprus

1100 B.C.
1100 Greek-speaking Dorians move south from the Balkans to settle in Greece

1000 B.C.

BRITAIN

Phoenician ship sailing to Britain to trade for tin

Atlantic Ocean

FRANCE

Mining tin

Hannibal
In 218 B.C. the Carthaginian general Hannibal crossed the Alps to surprise his Roman enemies during the Second Punic War.

Pyrenees

A L P S

ITALY

Massilia

The Etruscans
The Etruscans—the major force in central Italy—ruled Rome before it became a republic in 509 B.C.

Corsica

ROME

Adriatic Sea

Mediterranean Sea

SPAIN

Mining silver

Rome
Rome was originally a series of hilltop villages that gradually joined together to become a single city.

Palma
Balearic Islands

Sardinia

Sulcis

Gades

Tangier

Lixus

Trading highly-prized Phoenician cloths

Cartagena

Trading ship traveling along African coast

Cartenna

Sicily

CARTHAGE

Carthage harbor
The Phoenicians established the trading post of Carthage in 814 B.C. It soon grew to become the most powerful nation in the Mediterranean.

Phoenician writing
The Phoenicians had an alphabet of 22 consonants. The Greeks added vowels, making the alphabet that we use today.

Peoples of the Mediterranean

For the people living close to the Mediterranean, the sea either presented a barrier that they could not cross or a wonderful opportunity to get rich through trade and conquests. The Greeks established trading colonies around the Mediterranean, while the Phoenicians were more adventurous and sent trading expeditions out into the Atlantic Ocean. The two peoples fought often. They were later joined by the Carthaginians in north Africa, the Etruscans from Italy, and, eventually, the Romans, who dominated the Mediterranean Sea and most of its coastline by 100 B.C.

Human sacrifice
The Carthaginians worshipped the sun and moon gods, offering human sacrifices during times of danger.

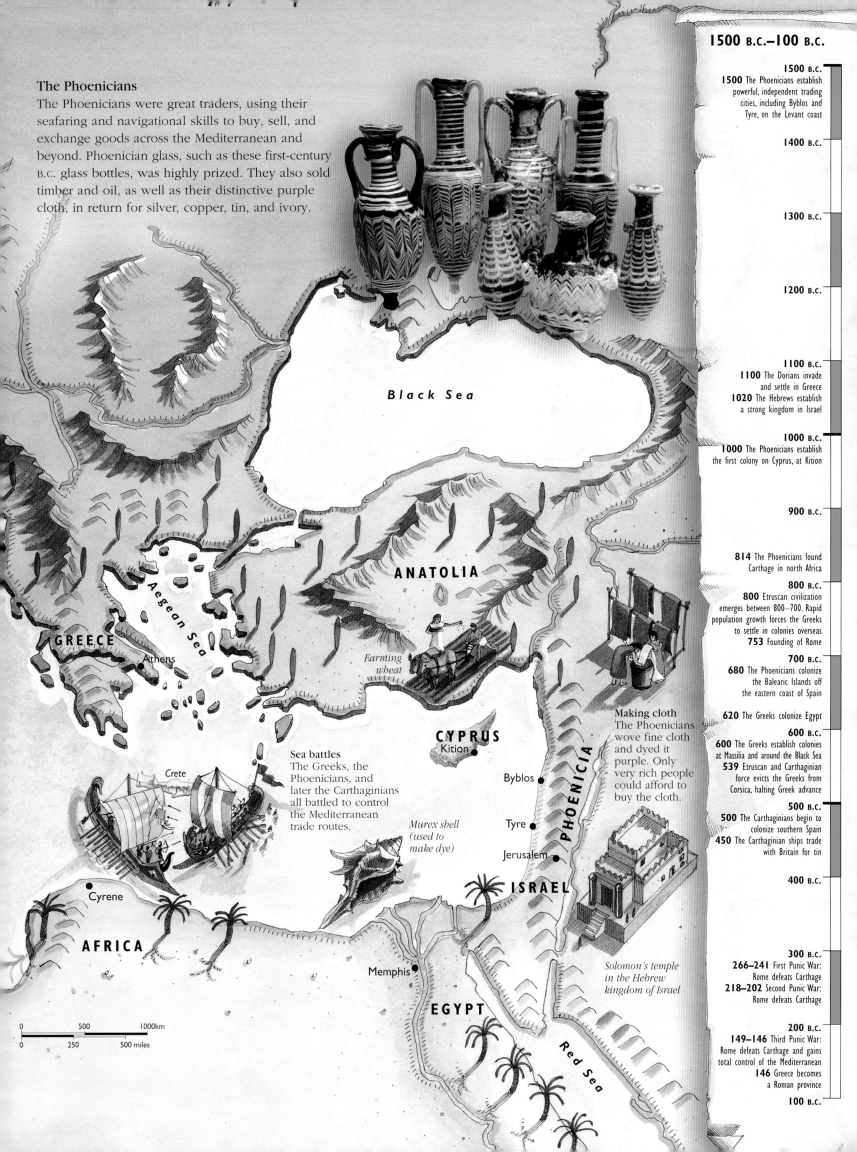

The Phoenicians

The Phoenicians were great traders, using their seafaring and navigational skills to buy, sell, and exchange goods across the Mediterranean and beyond. Phoenician glass, such as these first-century B.C. glass bottles, was highly prized. They also sold timber and oil, as well as their distinctive purple cloth, in return for silver, copper, tin, and ivory.

Black Sea

ANATOLIA

Farming wheat

GREECE

Athens

Aegean Sea

Crete

Sea battles
The Greeks, the Phoenicians, and later the Carthaginians all battled to control the Mediterranean trade routes.

Cyrene

AFRICA

CYPRUS
Kition

Murex shell (used to make dye)

Making cloth
The Phoenicians wove fine cloth and dyed it purple. Only very rich people could afford to buy the cloth.

Byblos

Tyre

Jerusalem

PHOENICIA

ISRAEL

Solomon's temple in the Hebrew kingdom of Israel

Memphis

EGYPT

Red Sea

| 0 | 500 | 1000km |
| 0 | 250 | 500 miles |

1500 B.C.
1500 The Phoenicians establish powerful, independent trading cities, including Byblos and Tyre, on the Levant coast

1400 B.C.

1300 B.C.

1200 B.C.

1100 B.C.
1100 The Dorians invade and settle in Greece
1020 The Hebrews establish a strong kingdom in Israel

1000 B.C.
1000 The Phoenicians establish the first colony on Cyprus, at Kition

900 B.C.

814 The Phoenicians found Carthage in north Africa
800 B.C.
800 Etruscan civilization emerges between 800–700. Rapid population growth forces the Greeks to settle in colonies overseas
753 Founding of Rome

700 B.C.
680 The Phoenicians colonize the Balearic Islands off the eastern coast of Spain

620 The Greeks colonize Egypt

600 B.C.
600 The Greeks establish colonies at Massilia and around the Black Sea
539 Etruscan and Carthaginian force evicts the Greeks from Corsica, halting Greek advance

500 B.C.
500 The Carthaginians begin to colonize southern Spain
450 The Carthaginian ships trade with Britain for tin

400 B.C.

300 B.C.
266–241 First Punic War: Rome defeats Carthage
218–202 Second Punic War: Rome defeats Carthage

200 B.C.
149–146 Third Punic War: Rome defeats Carthage and gains total control of the Mediterranean
146 Greece becomes a Roman province

100 B.C.

Black Sea

Scythian threat
Scythian archers were a constant threat to the Persian armies that defended the empire's northern borders.

• Pteria

LYDIA

The Royal Road
Riders carried messages for the Persian king along the 1,550-mile-long Royal Road.

Royal Road

Lake Van • Van

Assyrian power
The throne room of the king's palace in Calah was guarded by two huge stone lions with wings and human faces.

Caspian Sea

• Sardis

Tigris

• Carchemish

SYRIA

Assyrian kings
Kings of Assyria, such as Ashurnasirpal II, had great religious and political power.

Lake Urmia

MEDIA

The fatal blow
The Medes joined forces with Babylon to destroy the Assyrian empire in 612 B.C.

• Aleppo

■ NINEVEH
  Calah

• Assur

Cyprus

Chopping cedars for shipbuilding

Syrian Desert

ASSYRIA

• Hamadan (Ecbatana)

Keeping detailed records on clay tablets

Beekeeping

Assyrian warfare
The Assyrians were fierce fighters, besieging cities until they surrendered.

• Sidon
• Tyre • Damascus

Babylon
Nebuchadrezzar II made Babylon the most beautiful city in the world. He built a splendid temple with hanging gardens.

Euphrates

• Sippar

■ BABYLON

BABYLONIA

Zagros Mountains

• Nippur

■ SUSA

• Jerusalem

ISRAEL

• Uruk

JUDAH

Babylonian exile
Nebuchadrezzar II captured Jerusalem and took all of the Jews to Babylon as slaves.

• Ur

Messenger keeping the king informed about events

The great empires

Persian Gulf

For more than 600 years three great empires dominated the Middle East. The Assyrians were warlike and brutal, capturing or slaughtering their enemies. Their empire lasted for 300 years until the Babylonians, together with the Medes, captured the Assyrian capital of Nineveh in 612 B.C. The Babylonians turned Babylon into a fabulous city, but their power was short-lived. In 539 B.C. the Persians, under Cyrus the Great, seized Babylon and went on to create the greatest, most powerful empire that the world had ever seen. The Persian kings built beautiful palaces and became rich from trade and conquests, and their empire lasted for 200 years.

Red Sea

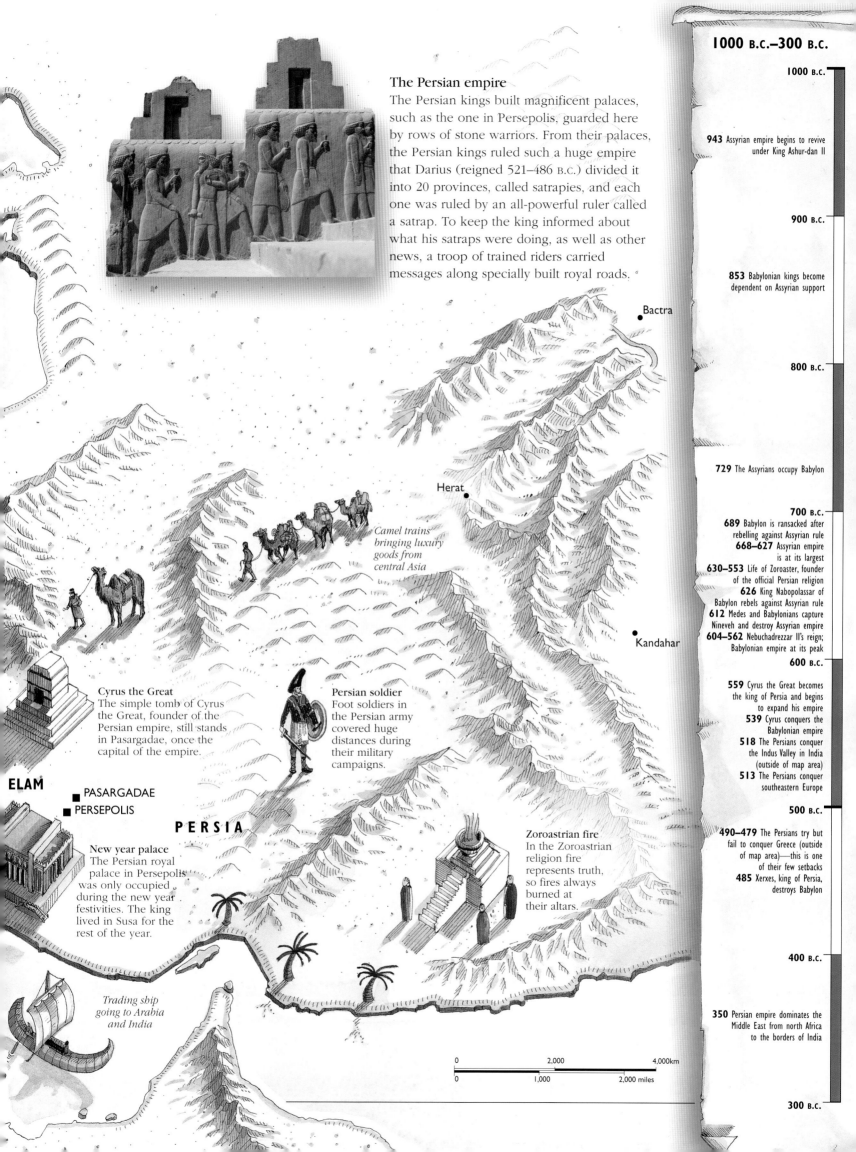

The Persian empire

The Persian kings built magnificent palaces, such as the one in Persepolis, guarded here by rows of stone warriors. From their palaces, the Persian kings ruled such a huge empire that Darius (reigned 521–486 B.C.) divided it into 20 provinces, called satrapies, and each one was ruled by an all-powerful ruler called a satrap. To keep the king informed about what his satraps were doing, as well as other news, a troop of trained riders carried messages along specially built royal roads.

Bactra

Herat

Camel trains bringing luxury goods from central Asia

Kandahar

Cyrus the Great
The simple tomb of Cyrus the Great, founder of the Persian empire, still stands in Pasargadae, once the capital of the empire.

Persian soldier
Foot soldiers in the Persian army covered huge distances during their military campaigns.

ELAM

■ PASARGADAE
■ PERSEPOLIS

PERSIA

New year palace
The Persian royal palace in Persepolis was only occupied during the new year festivities. The king lived in Susa for the rest of the year.

Zoroastrian fire
In the Zoroastrian religion fire represents truth, so fires always burned at their altars.

Trading ship going to Arabia and India

| 0 | 2,000 | 4,000km |
| 0 | 1,000 | 2,000 miles |

1000 B.C.–300 B.C.

1000 B.C.

943 Assyrian empire begins to revive under King Ashur-dan II

900 B.C.

853 Babylonian kings become dependent on Assyrian support

800 B.C.

729 The Assyrians occupy Babylon

700 B.C.
689 Babylon is ransacked after rebelling against Assyrian rule
668–627 Assyrian empire is at its largest
630–553 Life of Zoroaster, founder of the official Persian religion
626 King Nabopolassar of Babylon rebels against Assyrian rule
612 Medes and Babylonians capture Nineveh and destroy Assyrian empire
604–562 Nebuchadrezzar II's reign; Babylonian empire at its peak

600 B.C.

559 Cyrus the Great becomes the king of Persia and begins to expand his empire
539 Cyrus conquers the Babylonian empire
518 The Persians conquer the Indus Valley in India (outside of map area)
513 The Persians conquer southeastern Europe

500 B.C.

490–479 The Persians try but fail to conquer Greece (outside of map area)—this is one of their few setbacks
485 Xerxes, king of Persia, destroys Babylon

400 B.C.

350 Persian empire dominates the Middle East from north Africa to the borders of India

300 B.C.

MACEDON

Mount Olympus
The Greeks believed that their gods and goddesses lived on top of this holy mountain.

Mount Olympus

EPIRUS

Corcyra

Painted pottery
Greek craftsmen produced decorated pots, showing the gods or scenes from their history.

Ambracia

THESSALY

Horses were bred in Thessaly

Public speaking
Greek city-states were the first democracies. Politicians spoke to large crowds of citizens.

Thermopylae

AETOLIA

Priestess consulting the Oracle at Delphi

BOEOTIA

Delphi

Thebes

ATTICA

Marathon
Athens

Kephallenia

Olympic athletes
The ancient Olympic Games were held once every four years. Winners of each men-only event received a wreath of laurel leaves.

Sykyon
Megara

ACHAEA

Corinth

Argos

Mantinea

Olympia

Tegea

Acropolis
Originally a fort, the Acropolis in Athens was a giant complex of shrines and temples that dominated the city.

Ancient Greece

Ancient Greece was the home of an impressive culture. It was the birthplace of democracy, and many Greek ideas and inventions in philosophy, theater, architecture, mathematics, and medicine still influence us today. Ancient Greece was made up of many independent city-states, which grew from the 900s B.C. Each one had its own laws and way of life. Each city had a marketplace in the center, and an acropolis, or fort, built on higher ground. City-states were competitive—they fought many wars and, although they formed alliances, they never united to become a country. Athens and Sparta were the most important city-states. Athens was a busy trading city, as well as the first democracy. Sparta was a military state, where all male citizens had to be warriors. Throughout the Greek world citizens built temples and theaters where they held festivals, involving plays, processions, and games.

ARCADIA

Sparta

Warrior state
The city-state of Sparta was known for its tough soldiers, called hoplites.

Mediterranean Sea

Kydonia

CRETE

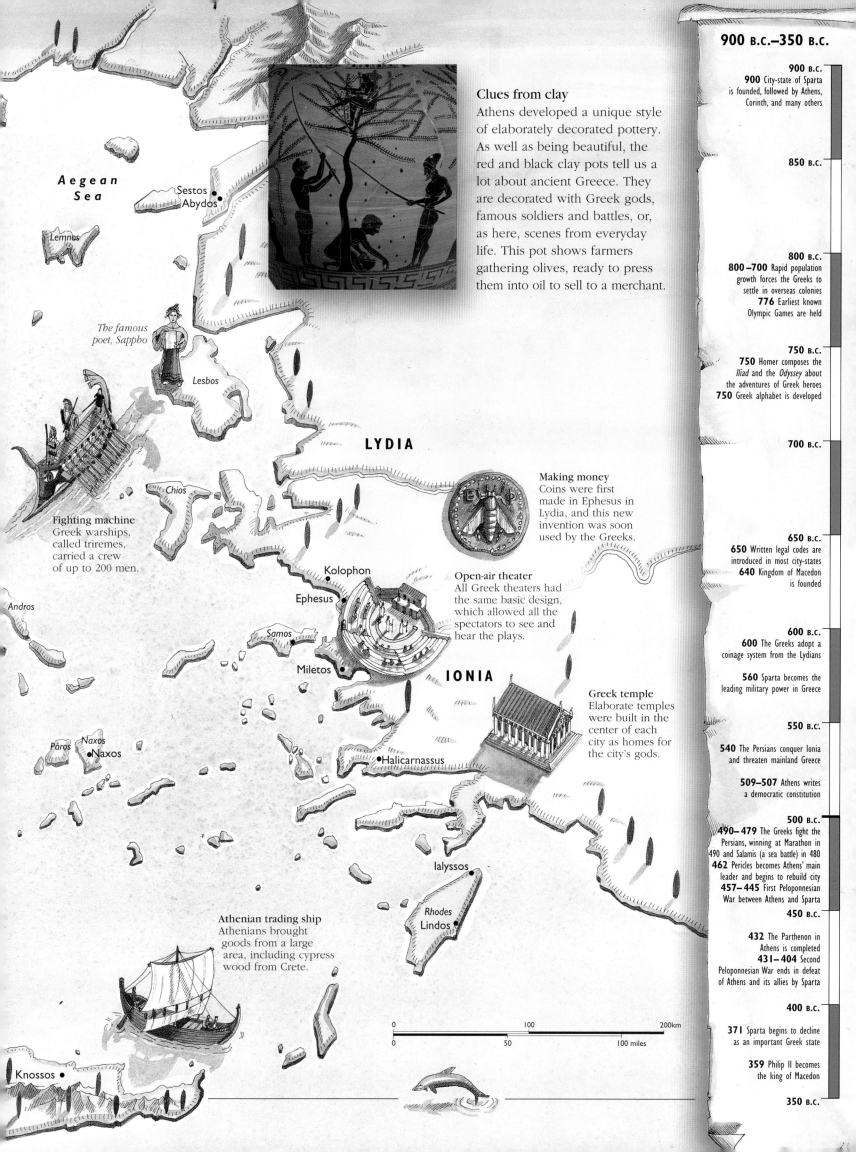

Aegean Sea

Sestos •
Abydos •

Lemnos

The famous poet, Sappho

Lesbos

Clues from clay
Athens developed a unique style of elaborately decorated pottery. As well as being beautiful, the red and black clay pots tell us a lot about ancient Greece. They are decorated with Greek gods, famous soldiers and battles, or, as here, scenes from everyday life. This pot shows farmers gathering olives, ready to press them into oil to sell to a merchant.

Chios

LYDIA

Fighting machine
Greek warships, called triremes, carried a crew of up to 200 men.

Making money
Coins were first made in Ephesus in Lydia, and this new invention was soon used by the Greeks.

Andros

Kolophon •

Ephesus •

Open-air theater
All Greek theaters had the same basic design, which allowed all the spectators to see and hear the plays.

Samos

Miletos •

IONIA

Greek temple
Elaborate temples were built in the center of each city as homes for the city's gods.

Paros   Naxos
• Naxos

• Halicarnassus

Ialyssos •

Rhodes
Lindos •

Athenian trading ship
Athenians brought goods from a large area, including cypress wood from Crete.

Knossos •

0   100   200km
0   50   100 miles

900 B.C.–350 B.C.

900 B.C.
900 City-state of Sparta is founded, followed by Athens, Corinth, and many others

850 B.C.

800 B.C.
800–700 Rapid population growth forces the Greeks to settle in overseas colonies
776 Earliest known Olympic Games are held

750 B.C.
750 Homer composes the *Iliad* and the *Odyssey* about the adventures of Greek heroes
750 Greek alphabet is developed

700 B.C.

650 B.C.
650 Written legal codes are introduced in most city-states
640 Kingdom of Macedon is founded

600 B.C.
600 The Greeks adopt a coinage system from the Lydians

560 Sparta becomes the leading military power in Greece

550 B.C.
540 The Persians conquer Ionia and threaten mainland Greece

509–507 Athens writes a democratic constitution

500 B.C.
490–479 The Greeks fight the Persians, winning at Marathon in 490 and Salamis (a sea battle) in 480
462 Pericles becomes Athens' main leader and begins to rebuild city
457–445 First Peloponnesian War between Athens and Sparta

450 B.C.

432 The Parthenon in Athens is completed
431–404 Second Peloponnesian War ends in defeat of Athens and its allies by Sparta

400 B.C.

371 Sparta begins to decline as an important Greek state

359 Philip II becomes the king of Macedon

350 B.C.

Ancient Greece:
The Greek world

From around 800 B.C., the Greeks founded trading colonies around the shores of the Mediterranean and Black seas. Greece's population had been rising for a while, but there was limited fertile land for growing the crops that were needed to feed everyone. Spreading out overseas solved this problem and made the Greeks richer at the same time. Some colonies were very successful, trading iron ore, tin, slaves, and wheat in return for wine and other goods. They also spread Greek culture and language throughout a wide region. By the 300s, they had declined in importance as other states, especially Carthage, threatened their livelihood. However, in 334 B.C. Greece's fortunes changed, when Alexander the Great invaded the Persian empire and made Greece the most important nation in the Middle East.

Greek culture
In their many colonies the Greeks built amphitheaters, such as this one in Miletos in southwest Anatolia (modern-day Turkey), in which to put on plays and sporting events. The success of these colonies spread Greek language, literature, law, religion, philosophy, art, and architecture far and wide throughout the Mediterranean world, especially in Sicily and the Etruscan states of northern Italy, and brought great wealth back to Greece itself.

Alexander the Great
Alexander the Great was born in Macedonia, northern Greece, in 356 B.C. He became king after the death of his father, Philip, in 336 B.C., and after a series of epic marches and remarkable victories he conquered the Persian empire. Although his empire fell apart after his death in 323 B.C., it left a lasting legacy of Greek cultural influence, known as Hellenism, that dominated the Mediterranean and the Middle East until the coming of Islam during the A.D. 600s. This coin shows Alexander wearing an elephant-scalp headdress to commemorate his victories in India.

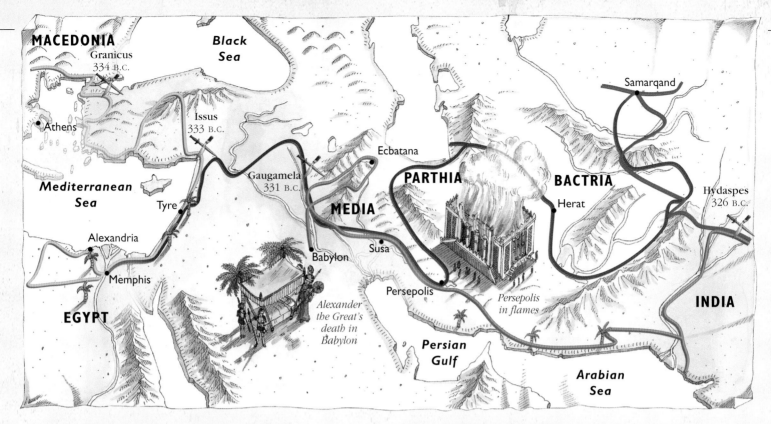

Map labels:

MACEDONIA
Granicus 334 B.C.
Black Sea
Athens
Issus 333 B.C.
Samarqand
Mediterranean Sea
Tyre
Ecbatana
Gaugamela 331 B.C.
PARTHIA
BACTRIA
Herat
Hydaspes 326 B.C.
MEDIA
Alexandria
Susa
Babylon
Memphis
Persepolis
Persepolis in flames
EGYPT
Alexander the Great's death in Babylon
Persian Gulf
INDIA
Arabian Sea

Conquering the world

Alexander and his army crossed into Asia in 334 B.C. and defeated a Persian army by the Granicus river. He beat an even larger Persian army in Issus in 333 B.C. Having conquered Egypt, he headed into the heart of the Persian empire, defeating the Persians for the third time at Gaugamela. His march took him into central Asia—destroying the Persian capital, Persepolis, along the way—and then into India, where he achieved his final victory. He died in Babylon in 323 B.C., aged only 32.

Alexander's legacy

Alexander left an incredible legacy. His empire stretched from Egypt to India and into central Asia, and at least 20 cities bore his name. Alexandria in Egypt soon became one of the greatest cities in the ancient world. It boasted a massive library, which was said to contain all human knowledge at the time. In 2003 a huge new library (right) opened in Alexandria to commemorate this ancient library.

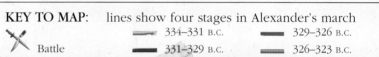

KEY TO MAP: lines show four stages in Alexander's march

✗ Battle

334–331 B.C. 329–326 B.C.
331–329 B.C. 326–323 B.C.

Alexander the Conqueror

Alexander was a superb military commander, leading his Macedonian troops into battle—often against overwhelming Persian strength. At the Battle of Issus in November 333 B.C. Alexander, seen here on horseback in the left of this mosaic, came face-to-face with the Persian emperor Darius, riding in a war chariot. After his army was defeated Darius was forced to flee the battlefield, leaving behind most of his family and a huge amount of treasures.

Roman Empire

The Roman Empire began life as a series of small villages next to the Tiber river in central Italy. According to legend, Rome was founded in 753 B.C., and in 510 B.C. the city became a republic. Over the next 500 years, Rome conquered all of Italy and then, after wars against Carthage, it conquered the lands that surrounded the Mediterranean Sea. Political instability led to the creation of an empire and a massive expansion of Roman power. The empire reached its greatest extent in A.D. 117 and enjoyed 300 years of relative peace and prosperity. Eventually, after civil wars and invasions, Rome became too weak to defend against invaders. By A.D. 476, the great empire had collapsed.

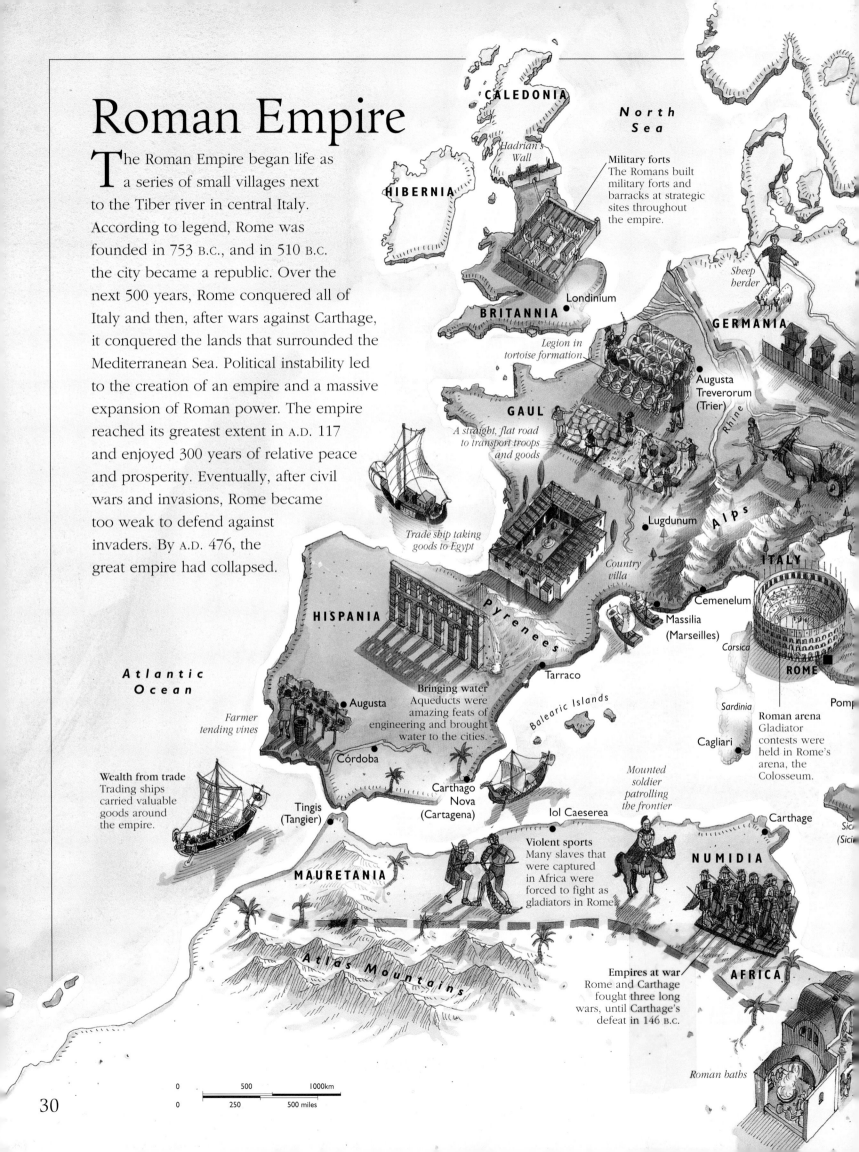

CALEDONIA

North Sea

Hadrian's Wall

HIBERNIA

Military forts
The Romans built military forts and barracks at strategic sites throughout the empire.

Sheep herder

Londinium

BRITANNIA

GERMANIA

Legion in tortoise formation

GAUL

Augusta Treverorum (Trier)

Rhine

A straight, flat road to transport troops and goods

Trade ship taking goods to Egypt

Country villa

Lugdunum

Alps

ITALY

Cemenelum

Massilia (Marseilles)

Corsica

HISPANIA

Pyrenees

ROME

Tarraco

Balearic Islands

Sardinia

Pom

Atlantic Ocean

Augusta

Bringing water
Aqueducts were amazing feats of engineering and brought water to the cities.

Cagliari

Roman arena
Gladiator contests were held in Rome's arena, the Colosseum.

Farmer tending vines

Córdoba

Carthago Nova (Cartagena)

Mounted soldier patrolling the frontier

Wealth from trade
Trading ships carried valuable goods around the empire.

Tingis (Tangier)

Iol Caeserea

Carthage

Sic (Sici

MAURETANIA

Violent sports
Many slaves that were captured in Africa were forced to fight as gladiators in Rome.

NUMIDIA

Atlas Mountains

AFRICA

Empires at war
Rome and Carthage fought three long wars, until Carthage's defeat in 146 B.C.

Roman baths

0	500	1000km
0	250	500 miles

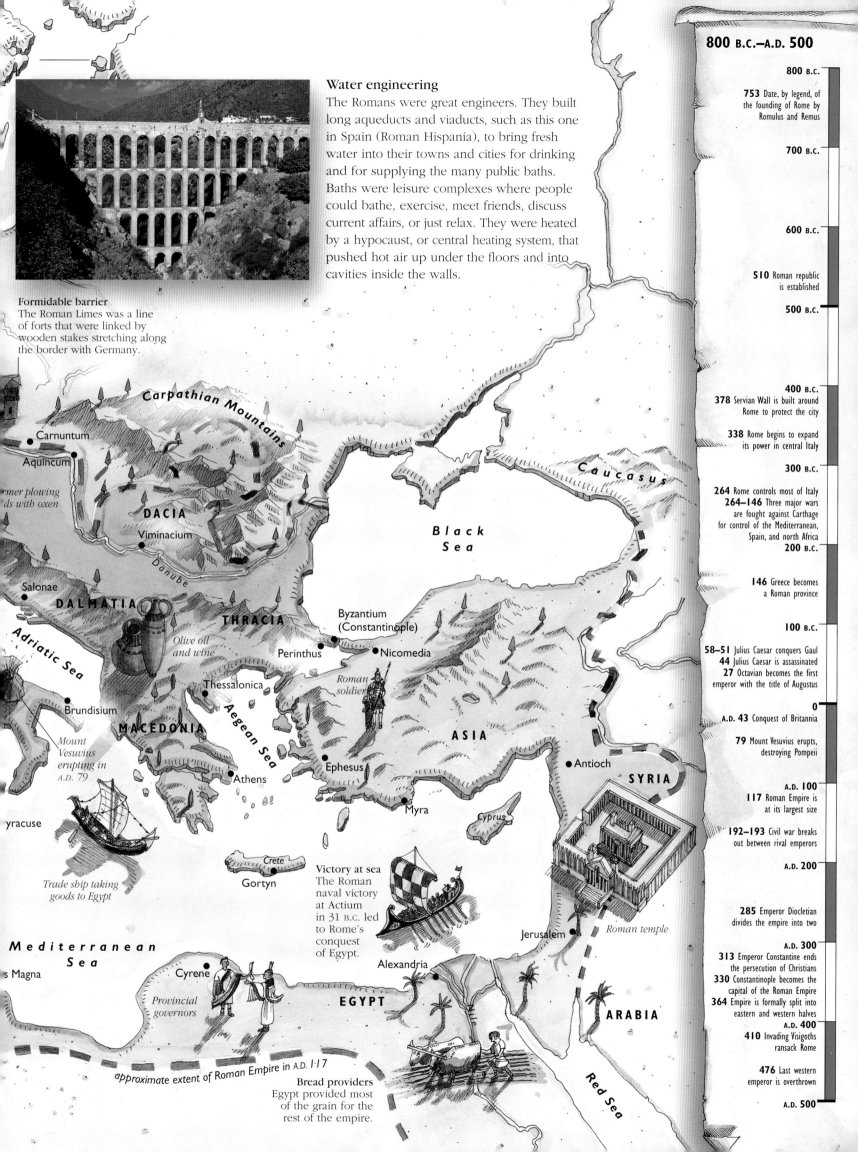

Water engineering

The Romans were great engineers. They built long aqueducts and viaducts, such as this one in Spain (Roman Hispania), to bring fresh water into their towns and cities for drinking and for supplying the many public baths. Baths were leisure complexes where people could bathe, exercise, meet friends, discuss current affairs, or just relax. They were heated by a hypocaust, or central heating system, that pushed hot air up under the floors and into cavities inside the walls.

Formidable barrier
The Roman Limes was a line of forts that were linked by wooden stakes stretching along the border with Germany.

Carpathian Mountains

Carnuntum

Aquincum

Caucasus

mer plowing
ds with oxen

DACIA

Viminacium

Black
Sea

Danube

Salonae

DALMATIA

THRACIA

Byzantium
(Constantinople)

Adriatic
Sea

*Olive oil
and wine*

Perinthus

Nicomedia

Thessalonica

*Roman
soldier*

ASIA

Brundisium

MACEDONIA

Aegean
Sea

Ephesus

Antioch

SYRIA

*Mount
Vesuvius
erupting in
A.D. 79*

Athens

Myra

Cyprus

yracuse

Crete

Gortyn

Victory at sea
The Roman naval victory at Actium in 31 B.C. led to Rome's conquest of Egypt.

Roman temple

Jerusalem

*Trade ship taking
goods to Egypt*

M e d i t e r r a n e a n
S e a

s Magna

Cyrene

Alexandria

*Provincial
governors*

EGYPT

ARABIA

approximate extent of Roman Empire in A.D. 117

Bread providers
Egypt provided most of the grain for the rest of the empire.

Red
Sea

800 B.C.–A.D. 500

800 B.C.

753 Date, by legend, of the founding of Rome by Romulus and Remus

700 B.C.

600 B.C.

510 Roman republic is established

500 B.C.

400 B.C.

378 Servian Wall is built around Rome to protect the city

338 Rome begins to expand its power in central Italy

300 B.C.

264 Rome controls most of Italy
264–146 Three major wars are fought against Carthage for control of the Mediterranean, Spain, and north Africa

200 B.C.

146 Greece becomes a Roman province

100 B.C.

58–51 Julius Caesar conquers Gaul
44 Julius Caesar is assassinated
27 Octavian becomes the first emperor with the title of Augustus

0

A.D. 43 Conquest of Britannia

79 Mount Vesuvius erupts, destroying Pompeii

A.D. 100

117 Roman Empire is at its largest size

192–193 Civil war breaks out between rival emperors

A.D. 200

285 Emperor Diocletian divides the empire into two

A.D. 300

313 Emperor Constantine ends the persecution of Christians
330 Constantinople becomes the capital of the Roman Empire
364 Empire is formally split into eastern and western halves

A.D. 400

410 Invading Visigoths ransack Rome

476 Last western emperor is overthrown

A.D. 500

Roman Empire:
The city of Rome

The imperial city of Rome—the capital of the Roman Empire—was by far the most grand and important city in Europe. It was a huge but often rundown city. The first emperor, Augustus (ruled 27 B.C.–A.D. 14), decided to make it beautiful, clearing away narrow streets and building public baths, theaters, and temples. He set up police and a fire service to keep its citizens safe and dredged and widened the Tiber river to prevent its frequent floods. By the end of the A.D. first century, Rome was a showcase for its empire, designed to impress visitors and enemies with the might of the Roman Empire.

Ruling the empire

From 27 B.C. to A.D. 476, Rome was governed by emperors. Some, such as Augustus, were outstanding, while others were brutal dictators or madmen. Below the emperor was the Senate—an unelected group of around 600 rich men that were called senators (below), who passed laws, controlled the treasury, and appointed governors to the Roman provinces that were not run by the emperor himself.

Street life

The streets of Rome were packed with shops that sold every type of produce. Bread was made in the shops themselves (above), while traders brought in fresh food and other goods from outside the city on handcarts and stocked up their shops each night, to be ready to sell the next day. Every street had a local bar, where wine and other drinks were sold, as well as many workshops, where everything from furniture and pots to fine clothes and jewelry were made. Although the main streets were swept clean, most of the smaller streets were very dirty, since people threw their garbage out of their windows. At night the city was pitch black, since there was no street lighting.

Women were separated from men and watched events from their own terrace on top of the building

City plan

In the center of Rome was the Forum—the political, judicial, and commercial heart of the city and the empire. There the Senate met to pass laws, and magistrates judged important legal cases. As the empire grew, successive emperors added new buildings to enlarge the Forum. The city also contained public baths, which were fed by water brought from outside the city by aqueducts, as well as many public squares and open spaces. A massive stone wall surrounded the city to keep it safe from attacks.

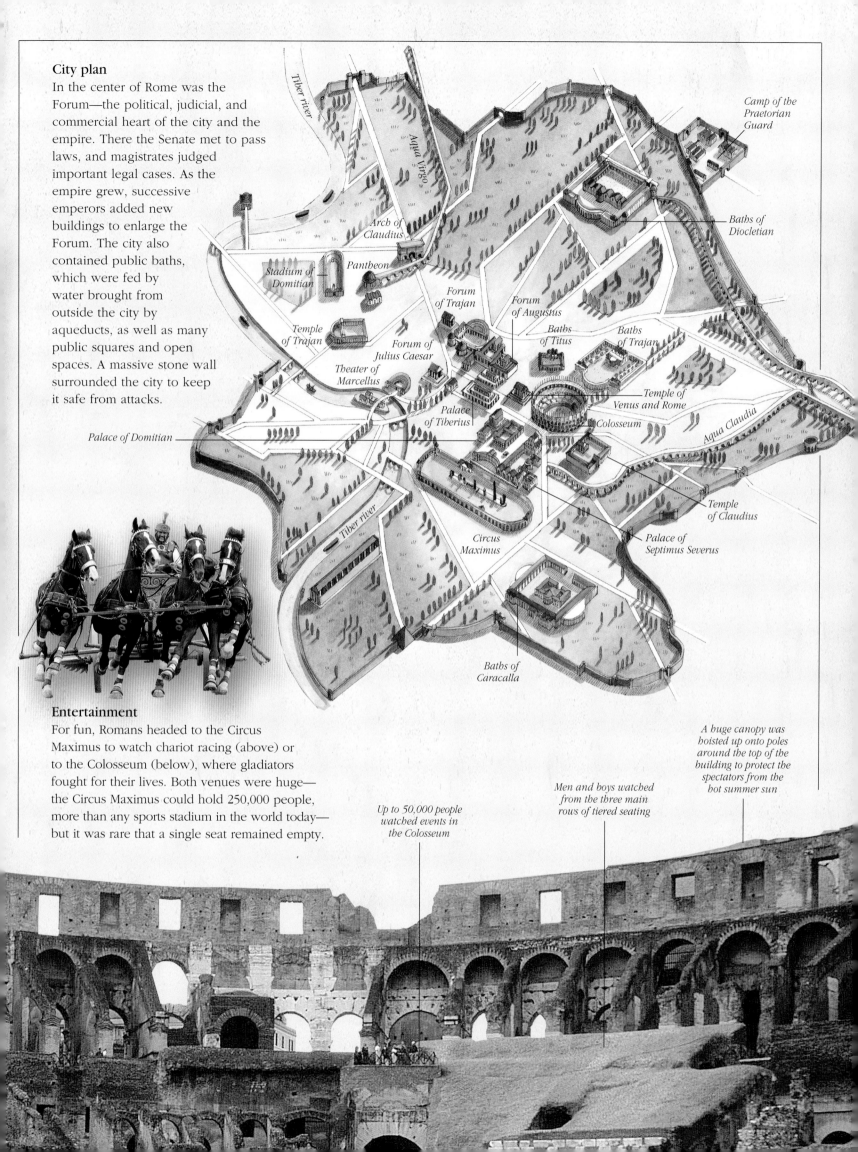

Tiber river

Aqua Virgo

Camp of the Praetorian Guard

Baths of Diocletian

Arch of Claudius

Pantheon

Stadium of Domitian

Forum of Trajan

Forum of Augustus

Baths of Titus

Baths of Trajan

Temple of Trajan

Forum of Julius Caesar

Theater of Marcellus

Temple of Venus and Rome

Palace of Tiberius

Colosseum

Aqua Claudia

Palace of Domitian

Temple of Claudius

Circus Maximus

Palace of Septimus Severus

Tiber river

Baths of Caracalla

Entertainment

For fun, Romans headed to the Circus Maximus to watch chariot racing (above) or to the Colosseum (below), where gladiators fought for their lives. Both venues were huge—the Circus Maximus could hold 250,000 people, more than any sports stadium in the world today—but it was rare that a single seat remained empty.

A huge canopy was hoisted up onto poles around the top of the building to protect the spectators from the hot summer sun

Men and boys watched from the three main rows of tiered seating

Up to 50,000 people watched events in the Colosseum

Ancient Africa

Around 5,500 years ago the grassy plains of the Sahara began to dry out and turn into a desert, dividing Africa in half. Until the introduction of camels from Arabia around 100 B.C., there was very little communication across this sandy desert. Many great civilizations flourished south of the Sahara. The oldest of these was in Nubia, close to the top of the Nile river. At one time the Nubian kingdom was so powerful that it ruled all of Egypt, but its successor, Meroë, was eventually conquered by the Christian kingdom of Aksum—the forerunner of modern-day Ethiopia. In the west the people of Nok learned to work with iron and produced beautiful terra-cotta figures. The neighboring Bantus were also skilled ironworkers, gradually spreading their language and technology east and south to everywhere except the far southern tip of Africa. In many places, however, Africans remained in the Stone Age, hunting and gathering their food from the forests and plains around them.

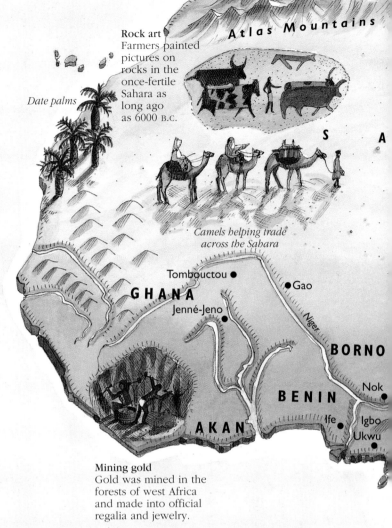

Rock art Farmers painted pictures on rocks in the once-fertile Sahara as long ago as 6000 B.C.

Date palms

Camels helping trade across the Sahara

Mining gold
Gold was mined in the forests of west Africa and made into official regalia and jewelry.

Atlantic Ocean

Nok culture

From around 500 B.C., Nok craftworkers produced beautiful terra-cotta heads and figures—among the earliest surviving artworks from Africa, south of the Sahara. They also learned to smelt iron ore to produce weapons and tools—a valuable skill when most of their enemies only had wooden spears and stones to use against them. Farther up the Niger River Valley was the city of Jenné-Jeno—the earliest-known town in sub-Saharan Africa, which became the hub of trade across the Sahara, and where traders used camels to carry gold, silver, ivory, and salt across the desert.

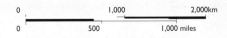

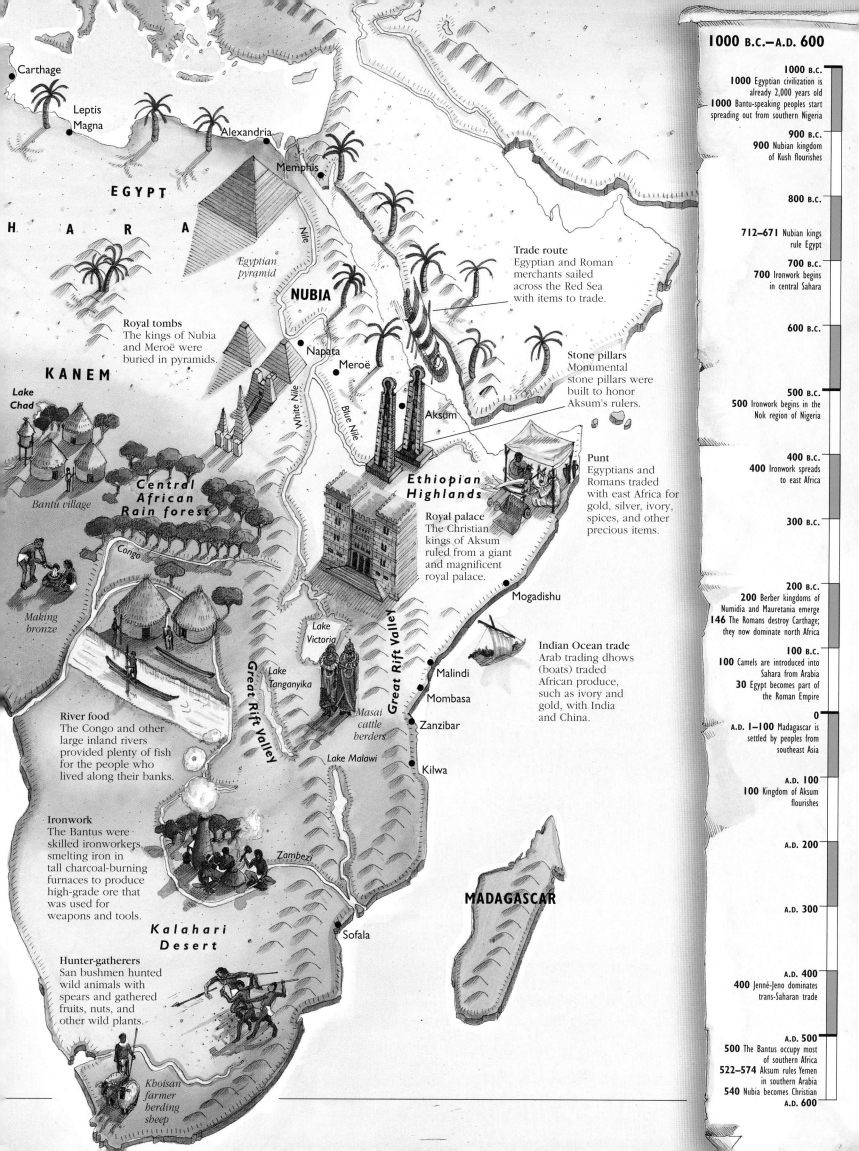

Carthage

Leptis
Magna

Alexandria

Memphis

EGYPT

S A H A R A

*Egyptian
pyramid*

Royal tombs
The kings of Nubia
and Meroë were
buried in pyramids.

KANEM

Lake
Chad

Bantu village

NUBIA

Napata

Meroë

Nile

White Nile

Blue Nile

**Central
African
Rain forest**

*Making
bronze*

Congo

Trade route
Egyptian and Roman
merchants sailed
across the Red Sea
with items to trade.

Stone pillars
Monumental
stone pillars were
built to honor
Aksum's rulers.

Aksum

**Ethiopian
Highlands**

Royal palace
The Christian
kings of Aksum
ruled from a giant
and magnificent
royal palace.

Punt
Egyptians and
Romans traded
with east Africa for
gold, silver, ivory,
spices, and other
precious items.

Mogadishu

River food
The Congo and other
large inland rivers
provided plenty of fish
for the people who
lived along their banks.

Ironwork
The Bantus were
skilled ironworkers,
smelting iron in
tall charcoal-burning
furnaces to produce
high-grade ore that
was used for
weapons and tools.

Lake
Victoria

Lake
Tanganyika

Great Rift Valley

Great Rift Valley

*Masai
cattle
herders*

Lake Malawi

Zambezi

**Kalahari
Desert**

Sofala

Hunter-gatherers
San bushmen hunted
wild animals with
spears and gathered
fruits, nuts, and
other wild plants.

*Khoisan
farmer
herding
sheep*

Malindi

Mombasa

Zanzibar

Kilwa

Indian Ocean trade
Arab trading dhows
(boats) traded
African produce,
such as ivory and
gold, with India
and China.

MADAGASCAR

1000 B.C.—A.D. 600

1000 B.C.
1000 Egyptian civilization is
already 2,000 years old
1000 Bantu-speaking peoples start
spreading out from southern Nigeria

900 B.C.
900 Nubian kingdom
of Kush flourishes

800 B.C.

712–671 Nubian kings
rule Egypt

700 B.C.
700 Ironwork begins
in central Sahara

600 B.C.

500 B.C.
500 Ironwork begins in the
Nok region of Nigeria

400 B.C.
400 Ironwork spreads
to east Africa

300 B.C.

200 B.C.
200 Berber kingdoms of
Numidia and Mauretania emerge
146 The Romans destroy Carthage;
they now dominate north Africa

100 B.C.
100 Camels are introduced into
Sahara from Arabia
30 Egypt becomes part of
the Roman Empire

0

A.D. 1–100 Madagascar is
settled by peoples from
southeast Asia

A.D. 100
100 Kingdom of Aksum
flourishes

A.D. 200

A.D. 300

A.D. 400
400 Jenné-Jeno dominates
trans-Saharan trade

A.D. 500
500 The Bantus occupy most
of southern Africa
522–574 Aksum rules Yemen
in southern Arabia
540 Nubia becomes Christian

A.D. 600

Ancient India

The first ruler to unite most of India was Candragupta, founder of the Mauryan dynasty that lasted from 321 to 185 B.C. His grandson, Ashoka, was a bloodthirsty ruler who was so shocked by the death of more than 100,000 people at Kalinga in 261 B.C that he converted to Buddhism, a nonviolent religion. Buddhism became an important religion in India. After the Mauryans lost power, India broke up until first the Kushans and then the Guptas reunited the country. The Guptas were devout Hindus and supported the arts and sciences. During their time the great Hindu epics of the *Mahabharata* and *Ramayana* were completed and mathematicians invented the decimal system and the concept of zero.

H i m a l a y a s

Market city
The city of Taxila had been occupied by Persians, Greeks, Mauryans, and Kushans, and became a major trading center

Taxila

UTTARA PATHA

• **Candragupta**
After Alexander the Great left India in 330 B.C., Candragupta drove out the troops he had left behind and seized the land.

• Kandahar

Indus

T h a r   D e s e r t

• Pattala

• Barbaricum

• Junagadh

Bull pulling carts of produce to the market

Growing rice in paddy fields

Watering the fields
Oxen were used to pull up huge barrels of water from deep wells to irrigate the fields.

A V A N T I

Narmada

• Sanchi

Great Stupa at Sanchi

Ganges

• Eran

Mud houses with thatched roofs

Buddhist propaganda
All over India Ashoka carved statements about the correct way of life on stone pillars and rock faces.

Buddha
The Buddha achieved enlightenment at Bodh Gaya around 528 B.C.

• Barhut

Sarnath

• Bodh Gaya

■ PATALIPUTRA
MAGADHA

Pataliputra
Pataliputra was the capital of Magadha and of the Mauryan empire. It was one of the largest cities in the ancient world.

Ganges

V A N G A

• Tamluk

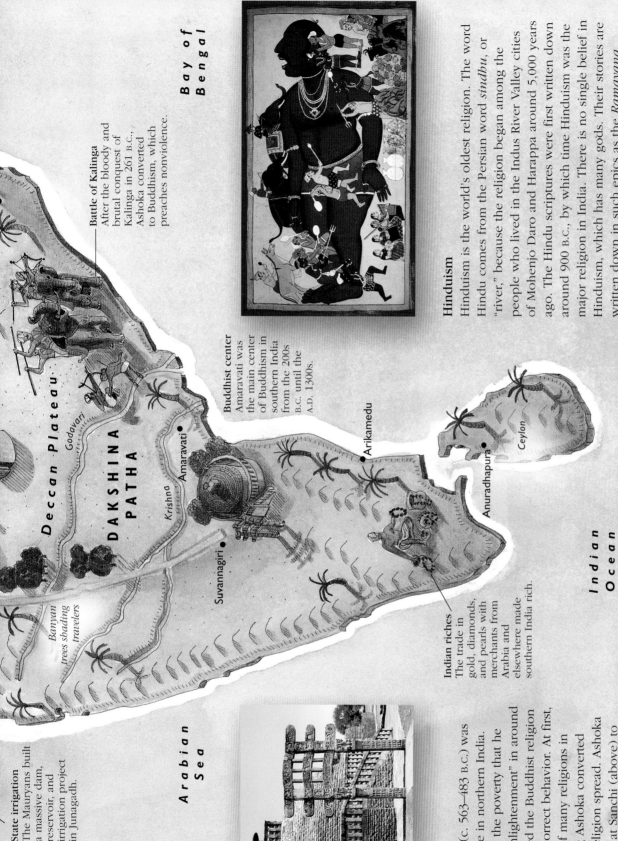

Hinduism

Hinduism is the world's oldest religion. The word Hindu comes from the Persian word *sindbu*, or "river," because the religion began among the people who lived in the Indus River Valley cities of Mohenjo Daro and Harappa around 5,000 years ago. The Hindu scriptures were first written down around 900 B.C., by which time Hinduism was the major religion in India. There is no single belief in Hinduism, which has many gods. Their stories are written down in such epics as the *Ramayana*, a scene from which is shown above.

Battle of Kalinga
After the bloody and brutal conquest of Kalinga in 261 B.C., Ashoka converted to Buddhism, which preaches nonviolence.

Buddhist center
Amaravati was the main center of Buddhism in southern India from the 200s B.C. until the A.D. 1300s.

Indian riches
The trade in gold, diamonds, and pearls with merchants from Arabia and elsewhere made southern India rich.

State irrigation
The Mauryans built a massive dam, reservoir, and irrigation project in Junagadh.

Banyan trees shading travelers

Deccan Plateau

Godavari

DAKSHINA PATHA

Krishna

Amaravati

Suvannagiri

Arikamedu

Anuradhapura

Ceylon

Bay of Bengal

Arabian Sea

Indian Ocean

Buddhism

Siddhártha Gautama (c. 563–483 B.C.) was born a wealthy prince in northern India. He was distressed by the poverty that he saw, and after his "enlightenment" in around 528 B.C., he developed the Buddhist religion of nonviolence and correct behavior. At first, Buddhism was one of many religions in India, but when King Ashoka converted to it in 260 B.C., the religion spread. Ashoka built the Great Stupa at Sanchi (above) to house the remains of the Buddha's body.

0   200   400
0   200   400 miles
0   400   800km

Ancient China

In 221 B.C. Zheng, the ruler of Qin in central China, defeated his rivals and united China. He took the title Qin Shi Huangdi, or "first sovereign Qin emperor." Ever since 1122 B.C., China had supposedly been united under the Zhou kings, but real power rested with the many provincial leaders, who often had more power than the king himself. Qin Shi Huangdi changed all of this by setting up a strong state where all power remained with the emperor. He built the Great Wall to keep out invaders, as well as many roads and canals. But after his death a civil war broke out, and the rulers of the Han dynasty came to power in 202 B.C. The Han expanded the empire south and east, but when they were overthrown in A.D. 220, China split into three kingdoms.

The Great Wall
The first emperor connected various state and city walls to form a single barrier that was 2,145 miles across the north of China. It was built from rammed earth and reinforced with brushwood.

Dunhuang

The Silk Road
Merchants used camels to carry silk and other valuable goods along the Silk Road, which connected China to western Asia and Europe.

Huang He (Yellow River)

Qin Mountains

Silk Road

Qin

Buddhism
In around A.D. 100 Indian monks brought Buddhism to China.

Growing tea in hilly areas

Terra-Cotta Army
When Qin Shi Huangdi died, he was buried with 7,000 lifelike terra-cotta soldiers to guard him in the afterlife.

Jiaozhou

Buddhism

The Buddhist religion was introduced to China by monks from India—one of whom is shown here with Buddha himself—around A.D. 100. The peaceful teachings of Buddhism appealed to the Chinese people during the troubled years after the fall of the Han dynasty in A.D. 220, and it soon became one of China's three major religions, alongside Confucianism and Taoism. The monks traveled into China along the Silk Road—a series of trade routes that connected the major cities of China with central Asia, the eastern Mediterranean, and eventually Rome. Merchants traveled along the road carrying silk, jade, and, much later, fine porcelain.

MONGOLIA

Nomads
Warlike nomads living on the grassy steppes of central Asia often threatened China and sometimes even invaded it. The Great Wall was built to keep them out.

Traders bringing furs from Siberia

Loulang

Teams of oxen plowing fields

Ji

Yinjang

Person doing calligraphy

Coin with a hole so that it could be kept on a string

Xinjiang

Huang He (Yellow river)

Linzi

Qufu

Farmers using foot-driven irrigation machine

Luoyang

hang'an

Royal palace at Xinjiang

Silk
The Chinese discovered how to make silk from the cocoon of the silkworm around 500 B.C. Only very important people were allowed to wear silk.

Gaixia

Nanjing

Huai

Yellow Sea

Wu

Chang (Yangtze)

Han

Boundary of Han empire

Ying

The Han dynasty
At the battle of Gaixia in 202 B.C. the Han ruler Gaozu established his supremacy over all of China.

Navigation
The Chinese invented the magnetic compass and used it to navigate successfully out at sea.

Planting rice in a paddy field

eeping control
he first emperor
urned the books
f scholars who
isagreed with
im and executed
is opponents.

Lingling

Papermaking
Paper was made by pulping and then drying and pressing the fibers from silk rags, bamboo, and mulberry bark.

Nanhai

South China Sea

Hainan

0   250   500km
0   125   250 miles

North American peoples

The first people arrived in North America from Siberia over the land bridge that existed around 17,000 years ago. They slowly moved south, spreading out over the vast plains, woodlands, deserts, and mountains of the continent, living as hunter-gatherers as they went. From around 700 B.C., the Adena people of the Ohio River Valley began to cultivate wild plants for food and build sacred earthworks and burial mounds. The later Hopewell people, who spread out from the Ohio River Valley into the Mississippi River Valley, built towns, burial mounds, and a huge earthwork in the shape of a snake—although no one really knows why they did this. The people of the southwestern deserts began to settle down into farming communities by around A.D. 300, eventually building complex villages of adobe (dried mud) brick houses. In the far north of America the Inuit people learned how to live in very cold conditions, trapping wild animals for their fur, meat, and bones.

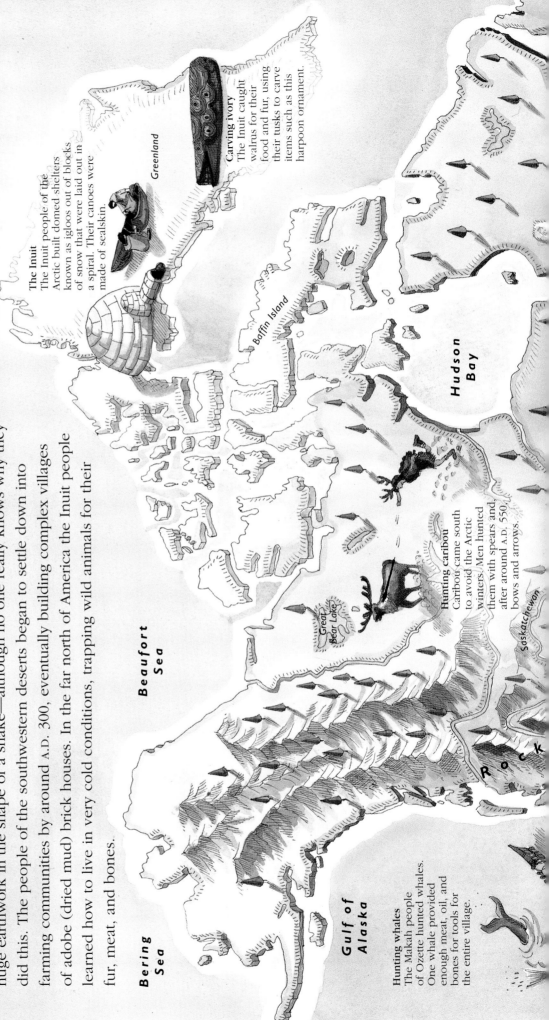

Greenland Sea

Greenland

The Inuit
The Inuit people of the Arctic built domed shelters known as igloos out of blocks of snow that were laid out in a spiral. Their canoes were made of sealskin.

Carving ivory
The Inuit caught walrus for their food and fur, using their tusks to carve items such as this harpoon ornament.

Baffin Island

Hudson Bay

Beaufort Sea

Great Bear Lake

Hunting caribou
Caribou came south to avoid the Arctic winters. Men hunted them with spears and, after around A.D. 550, bows and arrows.

Saskatchewan

Bering Sea

Gulf of Alaska

Hunting whales
The Makah people of Ozette hunted whales. One whale provided enough meat, oil, and bones for tools for the entire village.

Rock

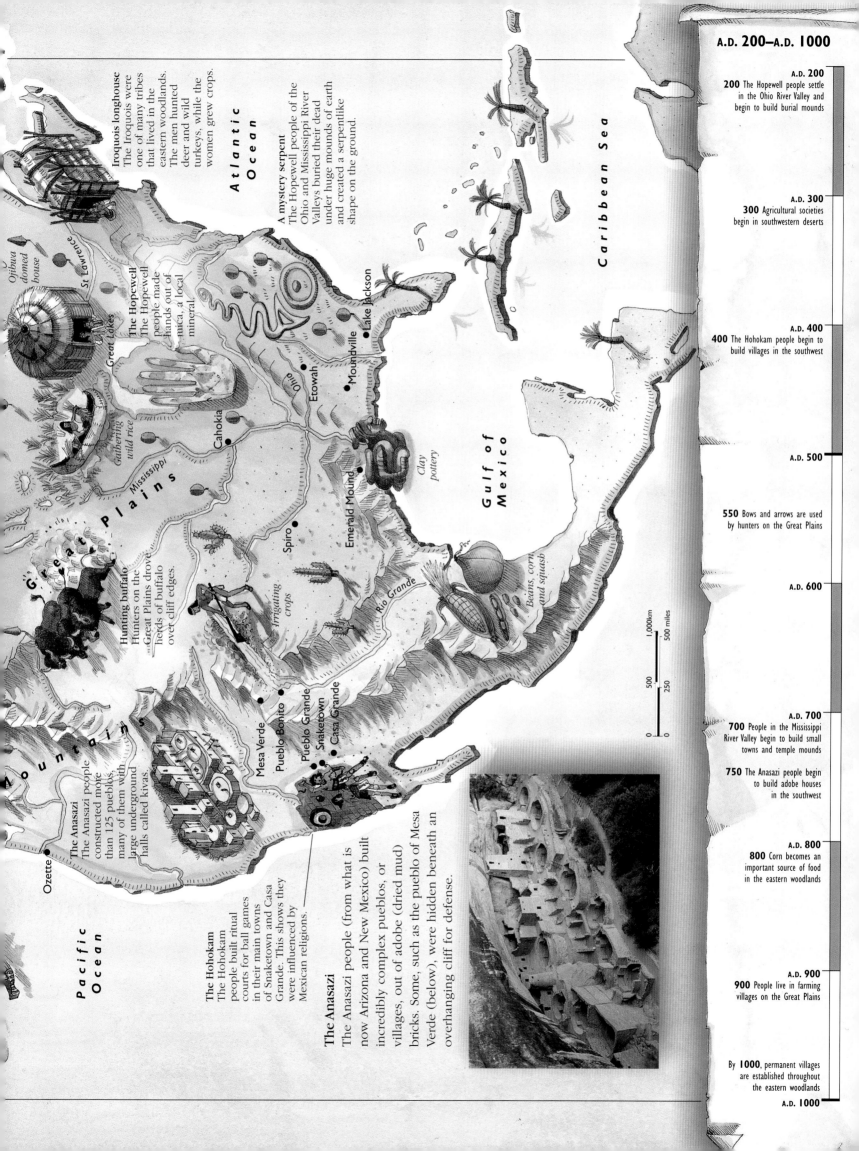

Atlantic Ocean

Caribbean Sea

Gulf of Mexico

Pacific Ocean

Great Plains

Mountains

Great Lakes

St Lawrence

Mississippi

Rio Grande

Ohio

Ojibwa domed house

Iroquois longhouse
The Iroquois were one of many tribes that lived in the eastern woodlands. The men hunted deer and wild turkeys, while the women grew crops.

A mystery serpent
The Hopewell people of the Ohio and Mississippi River Valleys buried their dead under huge mounds of earth and created a serpentlike shape on the ground.

The Hopewell
The Hopewell people made hands out of mica, a local mineral.

Gathering wild rice

Irrigating crops

Hunting buffalo
Hunters on the Great Plains drove herds of buffalo over cliff edges.

Clay pottery

Beans, corn and squash

Cahokia

Etowah
Moundville
Lake Jackson

Spiro
Emerald Mound

Mesa Verde
Pueblo Bonito
Pueblo Grande
Snaketown
Casa Grande

Ozette

The Anasazi
The Anasazi people constructed more than 125 pueblos, many of them with large underground halls called kivas.

The Hohokam
The Hohokam people built ritual courts for ball games in their main towns of Snaketown and Casa Grande. This shows they were influenced by Mexican religions.

The Anasazi
The Anasazi people (from what is now Arizona and New Mexico) built incredibly complex pueblos, or villages, out of adobe (dried mud) bricks. Some, such as the pueblo of Mesa Verde (below), were hidden beneath an overhanging cliff for defense.

1,000km
500 miles

500
250

500

0
0

A.D. 200
200 The Hopewell people settle in the Ohio River Valley and begin to build burial mounds

A.D. 300
300 Agricultural societies begin in southwestern deserts

A.D. 400
400 The Hohokam people begin to build villages in the southwest

A.D. 500

550 Bows and arrows are used by hunters on the Great Plains

A.D. 600

A.D. 700
700 People in the Mississippi River Valley begin to build small towns and temple mounds

750 The Anasazi people begin to build adobe houses in the southwest

A.D. 800
800 Corn becomes an important source of food in the eastern woodlands

A.D. 900
900 People live in farming villages on the Great Plains

By **1000**, permanent villages are established throughout the eastern woodlands

A.D. 1000

Central and South America

A series of ancient civilizations—most of them based around a single city—rose and fell in Central and South America between 1000 B.C. and A.D. 1000. The Olmecs built ceremonial pyramid earth mounds and carved huge stone sculptures. To the north of them the city of Teotihuacán grew larger than Rome and contained the biggest building in the ancient Americas: the Pyramid of the Sun. The major civilization in the region was the Maya, who built massive pyramid temple complexes and were skilled mathematicians and astronomers. In South America the Andean people built a huge stone temple mound with rooms that were filled with stone carvings of their gods. The Moche were skilled pottery makers, while the stonemasons of Tiahuanaco built huge temples and palaces.

Teotihuacán
The city of Teotihuacán started as a small village, but by A.D. 500, it grew to cover eight sq. miles and house as many as 200,000 people. At its center were the huge pyramids of the sun and moon.

Nose pendant (worn by nobility)

Olmec stone sculpture

Mayan men playing a ball game

Mayan temple
The Mayans built their temples on top of stepped pyramids. A new temple was dedicated to the gods by sacrificing prisoners that were captured during a war.

Mayan writing
The Mayans wrote with hieroglyphic picture writing. Each glyph represented a syllable.

Pyramid at Copán
Copán was one of the most important cites in the Mayan empire and flourished during the 600s. The ruler of Copán was buried in this step pyramid which dominates the city.

Gulf of Mexico

Caribbean Sea

Pacific Ocean

Andes

Weaving with alpaca and llama wool

Chichén Itzá

Tikal

Copán

Jaguar

Yucatán Peninsula

Palenque

San Lorenzo

Tres Zapotes

Teotihuacán

Monte Albán

Wild turkey kept for food

Jade necklace from Teotihuacán

Fishing from a reed boat

Fishing on Lake Titicaca

Steep hillsides terraced and irrigated for farming

Andes

Lake Titicaca

Tiahuanaco

Alto Rairez

Gold panning in Andean streams

Huarpa

Huari

Nazca

Pampa Ingenio

Corn grown in irrigated fields

Moche

Pañamarca

Viracocha

Pampa Grande

Cerro Vicus

Moche

Moche warrior graves

San Pedro de Atacama

Nazca Lines
The Nazca people drew huge geometric shapes and outlines of animals, birds, and insects in the desert sands.

Tiahuanaco
The highest city in the Andes controlled a large empire. At its heart was a precinct of temples and palaces, as well as the stone Gateway of the Sun.

Moche—the capital of the Moche state—contained two huge adobe (mud brick) platforms that were dedicated to the sun and moon, as well as a vast royal burial site.

The Maya
The Maya settled in Central America from around 1000 B.C. They began to build temple pyramids on which to worship their gods, and by 350 B.C., they were creating powerful city-states such as Palenque, Tikal, and Copán. The Maya created the only complete picture writing system in the ancient Americas. It was a sophisticated system that could fully express their entire spoken language. They were also skilled mathematicians and studied the stars so that they could draw up a detailed calendar that told them when eclipses of the sun and moon occurred.

Mayan city-states dominated the region from A.D. 300 to 800, but then they went into decline for reasons that no one fully understands today. The exception was the northern city of Chichén Itzá, founded in around A.D. 850, which was dominated by the El Castillo pyramid, shown above. Eventually Chichén Itzá itself declined and was overrun by the Toltecs, which brought Mayan civilization to an end.

The Nazca
The Nazca people, like many other peoples in South America, were skilled potters, creating this beautiful painted vase showing men hunting vicuña, a llamalike animal. The Nazca lived in the coastal plains of Peru, much of which was hot, dry desert. There, they scratched shapes into the sand, including giant outlines of figures such as a spider, a hummingbird, and a monkey, as well as geometric shapes. These shapes are so big that they can only be fully seen from the sky. No one really knows why the Nazca created these shapes.

1,000 km
500 miles

500 B.C.–A.D. 1000

500 B.C.
500 Olmec civilization flourishes by the Gulf of Mexico
450 Monte Albán is the center of Zapotec culture

400 B.C.
400 Chavin de Huantar culture spreads throughout central Andes
350 First Maya city-state is built in the Yucatán Peninsula

300 B.C.
300 Olmec civilization declines

200 B.C.
200 City of Teotihuacán is founded
200 The Nazcas begin to draw lines in the Peruvian desert
150 The Maya first develop their picture writing around this time

100 B.C.
100 Moche state is created in northern Peru

0

A.D. 100
150 Pyramid of the Sun is built in Teotihuacán

A.D. 200
200 People in Huarpa begin to terrace and irrigate the Andes for agriculture

A.D. 300
300 Moche state is at its most powerful

A.D. 400
450 Tikal is the main Mayan city-state

A.D. 500
500 Huari state begins to create an empire in the central Andes

A.D. 600
600 Tiahuanaco empire dominates southern Andes region

A.D. 700
700 Huari empire overruns Moche
700 Teotihuacán is ransacked by armies from nearby rival city

A.D. 800
800 Mayan city-states begin to decline
850 Chichén Itzá, the last major Mayan city-state, is founded

A.D. 900
900 Center of Mayan civilization moves north to Chichén Itzá
950 The Toltecs migrate from Mexico and overrun the remaining Mayan city-states

A.D. 1000

Australia and Polynesia

Around 40,000 years ago nomadic peoples from southeast Asia arrived and settled in Australia. These Aborigines—the name we give to the original inhabitants of a country—were hunter-gatherers and, aside from in the far north of Australia, remained isolated from the rest of the world until the A.D. 1700s. The Polynesians gradually settled on the isolated islands of the Pacific Ocean in one of the most extraordinary feats of exploration in human history. With no navigational aids, except for the the sun and the stars, they sailed their canoes over vast expanses of ocean, observing wind and wave patterns, the formation of clouds, and the flight of birds, in order to locate islands that were hidden over the horizon. By A.D. 1000, they had reached their final destination— Aotearoa, the islands we now call New Zealand.

North Pacific Ocean

Eating well
Polynesians kept chickens, dogs, and pigs, grew bananas, breadfruit, sweet potatoes, yams, and other crops.

Coral Sea

Gulf of Carpentaria

Living in the sky
Aborigines living on the swampy coastline built raised huts to protect themselves from snakes.

Great Sandy Desert

People telling dreamtime stories

Grinding grass seeds between stones for food

Ayers Rock

Ayers Rock
This giant rock has always been a sacred place for Aborigines. There, and at other sacred sites, they would perform dances, accompanied by a didgeridoo.

A U S T R A L I A

Great Dividing Range

Hunting for turtles using outrigger canoes

Hunting kangaroos
Aborigines hunted kangaroos for their meat with spears and boomerangs— curved sticks that returned when they were thrown.

Searching for edible roots

Digging a well for water

Darling

Lachlan

Murray

Fishing with nets in eastern rivers

Great Australian Bight

Tasman Sea

Collecting seashells to trade for other items

Tasmania

| 0 | | 1,000 | | 2,000km |
| 0 | 500 | | 1,000 miles | |

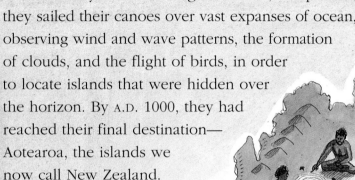

Oceangoing canoes
The twin-hulled, oceangoing canoes were up to 98 feet long and could carry up to 200 people, as well as supplies for the journey, animals, and seeds to plant on their new island home.

Gilbert Islands

Tuvalu

Solomon Islands

Sturdy ships
Polynesian canoes were made from dug-out tree trunks with sails made of palm leaf matting and had outriggers to stabilize them; the ropes were made from coconut fibers.

Vanuatu

Weaving baskets

Samoa

Smaller canoes were used for fishing between the local islands

Fiji

Catching coconuts from palm trees

Tonga

Cook Islands

Tahiti

New Caledonia
Harvesting yams

S o u t h
P a c i f i c
O c e a n

Long-distance voyages
Oceangoing canoes had to sail at least 1,550 miles across the open sea to reach Aotearoa.

The Maori
The Polynesian settlers in Aotearoa became known as Maori. Their warriors fought each other using sharp-edged clubs that were made out of whalebone.

Carving wood
The Maori carved statues of Pukaki, one of their main ancestors, out of wood.

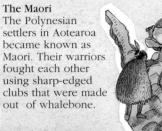

AOTEAROA

Hunting moa (a flightless bird)

Dreamtime
Aborigines believe that their ancestors were heroes who walked the earth during Tjukurpa, or dreamtime. Some ancestors were human, some were animals and plants, and others were the sun, stars, wind, and rain. They used certain paths that link the land and the people together. Aborigines retell the stories of dreamtime from generation to generation, using paintings on rocks and walking along the sacred paths.

500 B.C.
500 Aborigines are already well established in Australia and the Solomon Islands

400 B.C.

300 B.C.
300 Polynesian culture develops in Fiji, Samoa, and Tonga

200 B.C.
200 The Polynesians sail east to the Cook Islands and Tahiti

100 B.C.

0

A.D. 100

A.D. 200

A.D. 300
300 The Polynesians reach distant Easter Island in the eastern Pacific Ocean (not shown on map area)

A.D. 400
400 The Polynesians sail north from the Marquesas Islands to settle in the Line Islands and Hawaii (not shown on map area)

A.D. 500

A.D. 600

A.D. 700

A.D. 800

A.D. 900
900s The Polynesians sail south to settle in Aotearoa (New Zealand), where they are known as Maori, and eventually the Chatham Islands
A.D. 1000

Index

This index lists the main peoples, places, and topics that you will find in the text in this book. It is not a full index of all the place names and physical features that are found on the maps.

Acknowledgments

The publisher would like to thank the following for permission to reproduce their material. Every care has been taken to trace copyright holders. However, if there have been unintentional omissions or failure to trace copyright holders, we apologize and will, if informed, endeavor to make corrections in any future edition.

Key: *b* = bottom, *c* = center, *l* = left, *r* = right, *t* = top

Cover Aztec calendar The National Museum of Anthropology, Mexico City, Mexico; *Parthenon* with the kind permission of the Trustees of the British Museum, London, U.K.; 6*tr* Alamy/Walter Bibikow/Jon Arnold Images; 6*b* Walter Bibikow/Photolibrary.com; 7*tl* Alamy; 7*tc* The Art Archive/Musée du Louvre, Paris, France/Dagli Orti; 7*tr* The Art Archive/Archaeological Museum, Tikal, Guatemala/Dagli Orti; 7*bc* Corbis/Alfred Ko; 7*br* Corbis/SABA/Ricki Rosen; 9 Corbis/SABA/David Butow; 11 The Art Archive/British Museum; 13 The Art Archive/Dagli Orti; 14*tr* Corbis/Sandro Vannini; 14*b* The Art Archive/ Musée du Louvre, Paris/Dagli Orti; 15*t* The Art Archive/Musée du Louvre, Paris/Dagli Orti; 15*b* Corbis; 17 Corbis/Adam Woolfitt; 19 The Art Archive/National Museum, Karachi, Pakistan/Dagli Orti; 21 The Art Archive/Dagli Orti; 23 The Art Archive/Private Collection, Beirut, Lebanon/Dagli Orti; 25 Corbis; 27 Bridgeman British Museum; 28*tr* The Art Archive; 28*b* Corbis/Archivo Iconografico, South Africa; 29*c* Getty/Giulio Andreini; 29*b* The Art Archive/Archaeological Museum, Naples, Italy; 31 Corbis/Andrew Brown, Ecoscene; 32*tr* The Art Archive/Archaeological Museum, Naples; 32*l* The Art Archive/Museo della Civilta Romana, Rome, Italy; 32–33*b* The Art Archive/Joseph Martin; 33*cl* Corbis/Reuters; 34 Werner Forman Archive; 37 *Sanchi* Alamy/Profimedia; 37 *Ramayana* The Art Archive/British Library; 38 The Art Archive/Musée Guimet, Paris, France; 41 Corbis/Kevin Fleming; 43 *Chichén Itzá* Corbis/Michele Westmorland; 43 *Nazca pot* The Art Archive/Amano Museum, Lima, Peru; 45 Corbis/ Michael S. Yamashita

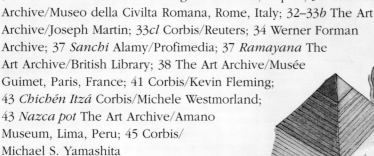